THE BATTLE SCARRED JOURNEY

Kim Wheeler

TotalRecall Publications, Inc.
1103 Middlecreek
Friendswood, Texas 77546
281-992-3131   281-482-5390 Fax
www.totalrecallpress.com

All rights reserved. Except as permitted under the United States Copyright Act of 1976, No part of this publication may be reproduced, stored in a retrieval system, or transmitted in any form or by any means electronic or mechanical or by photocopying, recording, or otherwise without prior permission of the publisher. Exclusive worldwide content publication / distribution by TotalRecall Publications, Inc.

Copyright © 2014 by: Kim Wheeler
All rights reserved

ISBN: 978-1-59095-184-2
UPC: 6-43977-41840-1

Library of Congress Control Number: 2013952276

Printed in the United States of America with simultaneous printings in Australia, Canada, and United Kingdom.

FIRST EDITION
1   2   3   4   5   6   7   8   9   10

Judgments as to the suitability of the information herein is the purchaser's responsibility. Total Recall Publications, Inc. extends no warranties, makes no representations, and assumes no responsibility as to the accuracy or suitability of such information for application to the purchaser's intended purposes or for consequences of its use except as described herein.

The scanning, uploading and distribution of this book via the Internet or via any other means without the permission of the publisher is illegal and punishable by law. Please purchase only authorized electronic editions and do not participate in or encourage electronic piracy of copyrighted materials. Your support of the author's rights is appreciated.

To

Kathleen Hunter for giving me life

For

Doctor Elaine McWilliams whose help and understanding was invaluable

and

To all the friends who have supported, helped and loved me

I am forever grateful to you all

Kim

Foreword

It took me around five minutes into my initial meeting and assessment with Kim to make the decision that this was a man who needed and deserved someone to have faith in him. But not just that to be prepared to walk along with him through psychological hell, not for a few weeks, even months but for years. I don't think at this point Kim realized this.

Not that I was some kind of sadist you understand but I knew therapy would be brutal. His life had to this point, had been brutal, I knew this even before I knew the detail, before perhaps either of us had even uncovered the first hints of the full horror of it.

Therapy would not spare him if it would prove to be effective. I was sure Kim had no faith or trust in me at first, why should he everyone, or nearly everyone had let him down. His dogs were trustworthy but they weren't human!

But there was something in this first meeting that allowed Kim to at least contemplate someone may just be prepared to hear his pain. And hear it I did, so did he and often he heard it himself and connected emotionally with it for the first time in those sessions.

At times the physical and psychological pain was so intense Kim struggled to see the point of living at all. Yet time and time again he returned and we continued. The therapy itself was painful. There were times when our sessions broke all records for shortest ever! This was because Kim's anger and frustration with his life and other people was hard for him to manage, but he always returned the next time having reflected on his emotions and actions.

Kim's courage to face his past, the demons that lurked there, the unprocessed trauma, the physical pain and scars and to survive the rejection he suffered time and time and time again was awe inspiring. Awe inspiring from my perspective that he had not emerged from this life some kind of monster himself. Yes he was angry at times, yes he got frustrated and yes he could sometimes give an excellent impersonation of Basil Fawlty, kicking his broken down car in exasperation! But he was also compassionate, creative, funny and ultimately undefeated, he was still fighting to find a way out this hell, of changing his path.

Learning to love and care for himself and see the value in Kim was Kim's biggest challenge. But he also had to do this whilst coping with incurable and intractable physical pain.

I only walked alongside Kim for a very small part of his journey so I have a very small part in this story. Yet I have seen how much he has progressed since we first met and since our sessions ceased. I have seen how he has showed admirable determination to try and help others through sharing his own painful life experiences. He has done this 'warts and all' with a raw honesty that is breath taking, heart breaking, but ultimately 'awe inspiring'.

I have learnt so much from Kim and I know this has helped me in my work with other people. The most of important of which is that it is possible to live with pain, both physical and psychological and not to deny it or dismiss it, yet still live a life…

Dr. Elaine McWilliams – Clinical Psychologist

Introduction

Kim was born in University College Hospital, London, back in July 1954 and within a few days, my Mother deserted me. Now the reasons behind my separation from my birth mother are pretty vague, but I can share what I think or imagine what it must have been like for her, and the pressure she had to endure at the hands of the cold hearted uncaring bastards who saw my mother as nothing more than a poverty stricken slut. If you were single and pregnant in 1953 you were looked down upon, if you were single, pregnant and the colour of the child's father wasn't a perfect white British, you were looked down upon, if you were single, pregnant, had a coloured man's baby inside your womb and the child was brown skinned, you were not only looked down upon from the rest of the country you were also scum and if you would like to add that she was also unwell whilst carrying a half caste child, was also homeless, a long, long way from home, loved ones, your family and were offered absolutely no help with no benefits whatsoever whilst being treated like scum, the chances of keeping that child were two fold, slim and none. My guess is that she was, like a lot of other women in those days told, 'You give that bastard brown child up right now or we will send you to Hoxton Hall Mental Home'.

Even the strongest will in the world could not cope with the unthinkable amount of peer pressure from her supposed betters and was forced to have her child forcefully removed. I was also removed from the only mother I had, and all because society deemed it wrong to have a bastard half caste child, well that's the truth of the matter, and I at the tender age of just fifteen days was torn away forever from my poor sick mother's broken heart. I often wondered what the kind of cruel separation would do to a child and a man, well I know exactly how that feels, rejection is a cruel bastard of an emotion made even worse when it was forced by some repugnant, odious and prejudiced suit working in the odious, repugnant, prejudiced system. How do I feel about this? Well one word sort of sums it up, heartbroken, but I can assure you, I have a dictionary of a lot more.

I was then moved to a children's home in Lewisham, where I have very few memories, but the five years incarcerated would have an enormous effect on the rest of my life and probably caused more mental angst than all of the following years put together.

Children don't do alone very well and although we survive physically, mentally we hurt and this hurt never seems to go away. As much as I hoped that one day my past emotions would dissipate, it seems the complete opposite occurred. So I and others who were brought up this way are indeed, scarred for life. Not being loved is the obvious emotion but there are a lot more, such as not being granted attention except for the basic needs, which then shatters self-confidence and plants the seeds of distrust in others, and when continually provoked that leads to strong feelings of violence, a longing for freedom and running away from a dull vegetated state while suffering from aloneness and loneliness, to happily jump through fire to find a friend, and sadly, be condemned to carry the odious suitcase of my past with me forever.

CHAPTER 1
…IN THE BEGINNING

Abandoned…

No Father to help and teach me
No Mother to hold me tight
No brothers or sisters to tease me
No one to say 'it's alright'
No playing in the gardens
No skipping through the woods
No going to the playground
I only wished I could
No one to hold me tight
When I'm frightened of the night
No one to hold and kiss me
No one to say 'goodnight'
No one to pick me up
When I fall down then cry
No one to show me love
No matter how I try
No one to wipe the tears
Of sadness from my eyes
No hands to reach or touch me
Alone, I wonder why
And alone, I sit and cry…

I was born in University College Hospital, London, back in July 1954 and within a few days, my Mother deserted me. Now the reasons behind my separation from my birth mother are pretty vague, but I can share what I think or imagine what it must have been like for her, and the pressure she had to endure at the hands of the cold hearted, uncaring bastards who saw my mother as nothing more than a poverty stricken slut. If you were single and pregnant in 1953, you were looked down upon. If you were single, pregnant and the colour of the child's father wasn't a perfect white British, you were looked down upon. If you were single, pregnant, had a coloured man's baby inside your womb and the child was brown skinned, you were not only looked down upon by the rest of the country, but you were also scum. Add to all that, if you were also unwell whilst carrying a half-caste child; homeless and a long, long way from home, loved ones, your family; and were offered absolutely no help with no benefits whatsoever whilst being treated like scum, the chances of keeping that child were two fold - slim and none. My guess is that my mother, like a lot of other women in those days, was told, 'You give that bastard brown child up right now or we will send you to Hoxton Hall Mental Home'.

Even the strongest will in the world could not cope with the unthinkable amount of pressure from her supposed betters, and she was forced to have her child removed against her wishes. I was thus removed from the only mother I had, and all because society deemed it wrong to have a bastard half-caste child. Well that's the truth of the matter, and I at the tender age of just fifteen days, was torn away forever from my poor, sick, broken-hearted mother. I often wondered what that kind of cruel separation would do to a child and a man; well I know exactly how that feels. Rejection is a cruel bastard of an emotion, made even worse when it is enforced by some repugnant, odious and prejudiced suit working in that odious, repugnant, prejudiced system. How do I feel about this? Well, one word sort of sums it up: heartbroken. I can assure you, I have a dictionary of a lot more.

I was then moved to a children's home in Lewisham, where I have very few memories, but the five years of incarceration would have an enormous effect on the rest of my life and probably caused more mental angst than all of the following years put together.

Children don't do being alone very well and, although we survive physically, mentally we hurt and this hurt never seems to go away. As much as I hoped that one day my past emotions would dissipate, it seems the complete opposite occurred. So I and others who were brought up this way are indeed, scarred for life. Not feeling loved is the obvious emotion, but there are a lot more, such as not being granted attention except to fulfill basic needs, which serves to shatter self-confidence and plant the seeds of distrust in others. Being continually provoked leads to strong feelings of violence, a longing for freedom and a need to run away from a dull, vegetated state, all the while suffering from such aloneness and loneliness that I would happily jump through fire to find a friend. Sadly, it seems I was condemned to carry the odious suitcase of my past with me forever.

Perhaps just not having a Mother there to support me in the most important years of my life was utterly soul destroying. You are, after all, supposed to have a bond from birth. She did carry me for nine months but the emotional tie between Mother and child was cut not long after the physical cutting of the umbilical cord, and for the rest of my life I would not or could not, ever replace this Mother. Nor could the love, the bonded connection between us ever be found or replaced. The day she left me was the same day that I also lost love, which I have been searching for ever since, and suspect I shall go to my grave never ever finding the most important emotion every child deserves and needs, the one of a mother's love.

Kathleen…

> I don't know where you are
> Or the streets where you have been
> I don't know how your heart is feeling
> Or the pain that you have seen
> I don't know what happened to your soul
> Or if you're suffering giving me away
> I don't know how many sleepless nights you have
> How you've survived from day to day
> I don't know if you called out my name
> Or were so beaten back with shame
> I don't know if you ever loved me
> Or felt the pain of guilt and shame
> Kathleen, you are still my beautiful Mother
> I have loved you everyday
> I just wanted you to hear me say
> That I forgave you my beautiful Mother
> Forgiven you in every way.

So on my own as a newborn, I was fed and washed, but unfortunately the nurses never stayed long enough for me to have any type of real relationship or emotional ties. They were here one day and gone the next, and at my tender age, I needed exactly what I wasn't getting - to be loved, touched, caressed, kissed, held and even wanted.

The first few years came and went and so too some memories. The few that I have seem to have dulled with time or have perhaps been changed or made up by an overactive and bored mind.

I remember a bird flying through the window while we slept in our cots. I am unsure, but would imagine that there were at least ten cots per bedroom. Suddenly all the children woke crying and screaming in great fear and in the ensuing panic, the other kids lost it. It didn't seem to bother me; perhaps I was just too young to understand fear.

Another memory was being caught pissing on the floor and then being sternly told off by a fat woman who made me sit on a potty in view of everyone else. I remember thinking, 'Why get me to sit on a steel cold potty and piss more when I have already pissed all over the floor?'

Other memories are more hazy, like being given a football as a fourth birthday present that was immediately taken from me and put on top of a tall cabinet. I remember thinking again 'how bloody unfair life is', and that, sadly, the worst of all was the unimportance of tears.

Then once in a while we would all be herded into a room and told to sit on the floor whilst strangers would walk in and stare at us, whisper to each other, smile and laugh. One by one all my friends would disappear. I, however, seemed to be left behind... As the joke goes, 'I was so ugly I was fed by trebuchet', or perhaps, just perhaps, it was the colour of my skin, as I was half-caste and of unknown origin.

I grew up to have a great fear of strangers and I guess this is where it all began by being put on show like a rescue dog. I had absolutely no idea what was going on, but in time we all did. It was like we had to perform to get noticed - who could smile the sweetest, who could bully others and make it to the front of the queue for attention and grab the chance of a better life perhaps? I would sit and wait for instructions and wait and wait until someone thought I was suitable for their new home and lifestyle.

I'm a human boy child not a pair of curtains or a picture; I breathe, I bleed, I have emotions, I cry, and, yes, I even wet the bed, I'm scared, I'm lonely and alone, I'm frightened of all these strangers staring and grinning at me, I don't want to be an orphan.

I want my mum.

Mother Kathleen...

> The pain that drips
> From my innocent broken heart
> Fears of yet another day of empty loneliness
> Leaves me trembling in the dark
> Burning eyes, crying rivers of pain
> Red mist envelope my abandoned soul
> Never ever touching or seeing
> Mother Kathleen again

Solitude howls in the cold night air
Blindly I stumble
Hands held limp with sadness
Searching for something, that does not care
Is not there
That flew away like a dying leaf in a storm
That left me thinking
Wishing
I had never been born.

Somewhere, and at some time, during these formative years, something happened to me. What is unclear and, even as I write this after fifty eight years, all I have is a blurred, hazy memory of something I cannot be sure even took place. In saying that, it is a memory anyway of something that has lain dormant, hidden away in the dark recesses of my mind, that either won't allow me to remember the pain, or perhaps so brutal is this memory that it was just forgotten about since the hurt of it would or could destroy my life. It concerns molestation, perhaps insertion, and pain that I only truly faced and understood some forty years odd later.

I have stated that I already had a great fear of strangers and still today I have a fear, distrust, revulsion, a sick-to-the-pit-of-my-stomach hatred towards paedophiles and vicious anger towards revolting, slimy, unclean, smelly men who leered and still leer at me to this day. I find it very uncomfortable when eyed up by men, and any sort of inappropriate touching or fondling leaves me fit to kill. This comes from somewhere, but for the life of me, I just cannot remember when, or who or where, but I do know the fear arose in the first five years of my life. The only place this could have happened was in the children's home, and we all know there have been paedophiles abusing children since the day dot. I am not suggesting for one moment that this paedophilia was carried out solely by men; it might well have been a woman, but you know, somehow I doubt that as I have no fears of women – except only that of being attacked physically.

So how do I explain how I found out if the pain and the revulsion I felt was real or just a cruel joke or nightmarish dream? Well I will try my best to explain later on in this book.

Ugly Tree...

    I hit every branch of life's ugly tree
    Deserted in London, my mother didn't want me
    Fed by trebuchet because I was so very ugly
    Reared by the social that let every pervert touch me
    I'm so ugly,
    Rejected by my own kind, survival was the game
    Only thing I ever owned was my skin and a name
    My Mother was threatened with a mental home, was she really so insane?
    Her only crime was giving birth to me and was never to blame
    I'm so very ugly,
    My crime was just my colour as I wasn't a perfect white
    And as you swam around in paradise I drowned in a river of shite

For me there was only darkness, every hour was as black as night
And there was no one to teach the rules about being wrong and being right
I'm so very, very ugly,
Now I know about loneliness and I have shook the hands with pain
After many years on Planet Earth I still feel that I'm to blame
The freedom of life I was promised was attached to a ball and chain
There's one sure certainty, indifference will never change
Mother, oh Mother, why am I so ugly.

CHAPTER TWO
YOU'RE NOT WANTED

Some four or five years had elapsed when I was eventually picked like a performing dog in a circus of abandonment. Leaving for fostering was one of my unhappier memories. I didn't want to leave with those strange people, didn't want to leave the only home I had, so I held on to the pillars of the building for dear life. (Sadly I didn't run to a human being for comfort). One by one my tiny fingers were prised away from the sturdy pillar of my only home and I was unceremoniously dragged, kicking and screaming, and forcefully placed on to a green line bus to be delivered like a Pizza to my new life, my new foster parents. All alone, to await my fate. I found out some fifty odd years later how I was chosen. My unknown foster parents, who would one day be my adopted parents, were all gathered around their television watching a programme about dark skinned orphan children, when the notion struck them:

'Oh we should get one of those.'

Brown Skinned Boy...

They saw dark skinned orphans on TV
'We want one of those', so they ordered me
Brutally removed from my only home

Delivered to a new one, so lost and alone
Silently I was shown my cell sized room
There's nothing here to lift my gloom
On the bed was handmade teddy
'Would you like to play?' But I wasn't ready
I looked at the curtains, then down at the bed
Tears started to fall from my sweet little head
My only possessions were of fear and hope
I was just a child, how would I cope?
Lonesome and lonely I felt like running away
Crying in self-pity on my first day
I want my mum,
But she's not there
Alone and frightened, I wet the bed
'Plastic sheets for you', the angry woman said
I tried to do right but always got it wrong
Scratched the walls as my fingers bled, I sang a little song
Sugar in the morning sugar at night
Called horrible names I learn to fight
Caned at school my body wracked in pain
Told off at home and yes, beaten again
I scratched the colour from my skin
Because no one liked what I was wrapped in
Nowhere safe for this child to hide
So I kept these abuses hidden deep inside
As I could not cope with all the fear
Frightened of strangers, whenever they came near
I was still alone and very scared
I need my mum
She's still not there.

I eventually arrived at my new home unable to conjure up a sentence since one thing that does not happen in many nursery/children's homes is being taught etiquette and the Queen's English. I didn't know how to speak, just grunt and point and when angry I had already learnt the eye-fighting techniques of a hardened soldier about to fight to the death. I could burn through steel with my angry eyes and can still easily reduce grown men to trembling amoebas with my eye-fighting skills, honed to perfection as my vocal ability resembled that of a senile sheep rather than one of a five-year old human being. Most children of that age nowadays can recite Homers Iliad; I had problems just saying 'yes please' and 'thank you'.

I remember being taken into a sparse box of a room with curtains and bed covers that matched - steam trains and cars I think. There was a teddy on the bed that had been made by an aunt; it had buttons for eyes and I think it was the first time that I had seen one. I soon learnt how to throw it across the room in temper and bit by bit I managed to eat it, but I also learnt to cuddle it - the teddy was to become my best friend.

I also remember being shown around this large home and then later on standing in the dining room looking up at a Welsh Dresser that was so tall it seemed to reach the sky, and was full of many shiny and interesting things In my childish awe I pointed at everything and enquired innocently, 'Wat's that?'

'Don't touch; it's not yours,' came the overtly aggressive reply.

I was fostered for about twelve months and then finally legally adopted at age six. I don't remember if I ever returned to the nursery or if I just stayed with my new family. For some reason my name was changed to one I hated. Suddenly I was no longer Charlie but now Kim, which I absolutely hated. So not only was I laughed at while at school because of my background and the colour of my skin, now I had to endure even more bullying and taunts because of my new stupid name. I have often wondered how much name changes can alter a child's perspective of himself and his life and also how others saw me. Charlie was a normal British name; however Kim wasn't and it was also a girl's name.

I already had a great fear of strangers and my newfound hurt didn't improve my feelings towards adults and institution. Whenever I failed to do exactly what my Mother / Teachers told me to do, I would be caned at school by a bully of a headmaster, ordered to either bare my arse or hold out my hands. The very same thing happened with my new Mother at home, where again my bare bottom and legs were hit and slapped until red raw. I was shit scared of this woman and I began to hate her.

To prove a point let me tell you just one story.

It was early one summer evening and as usual I was in bed, lights out was always at 7 p.m. The early evening light shone through the flimsy curtains which made the bars on my window – yes, bars on my window, which silhouetted around my box room making it look like I was encased in a cage. I couldn't sleep because of the noise outside my window, so carefully I crept out of bed (a bit strange as no one could see me), moved the curtain half an inch and peered through the crack to see what was going on.

Sure enough my new family were all outside, laughing, joking and having fun. I wanted to join in. Suddenly my brother noticed the curtains twitch and saw me peering through the gap, and instead of waving or pulling faces he grassed me up. I read his lips as he said, Mum, Kim's up.

She turned and stared right at me. I froze with fear, knowing that I was in trouble and soon going to be hit, caned or just berated, or, if I was particularly annoying and she was having one of her 'Kim must obey' moods, all three punishments.

The back door slammed shut. Thud, thud, thud went her heavy footsteps as she climbed the stairs. I knew instinctively whether I was to be hit by cane or hands because if it was the cane I would hear her bedroom door creak open, then slam shut. Soon the thud, thud, thud of her heavy angry footsteps marched towards my bedroom, where I was now shitting myself, shaking with fear and wondering childlike at what was about to come through the sanctuary of my small bedroom.

Suddenly my bedroom door flew open, and there stood this angry monster towering over me, steam erupting from her ears and a three-foot cane in her hand.

'Hold out your hands,' she ordered angrily, 'and roll up your sleeves.'

I could hear my heart beating, louder and louder as beads of frightened sweat trickled down my innocent face as I slowly held my hands out and waited for the searing pain. I didn't have to wait long: three, four, five times, maybe more, the cane sliced into my trembling little hands. On other occasions she would hit my legs with the palms of her gnarled hands whilst verbally berating me to the rhythm of the slaps.

I screamed,

'Please mummy, stop!'

Don't hit me...

Don't hit me mummy
Please don't hit me anymore
My flesh is crying
I feel like dying
Please don't hit me anymore
I wipe the tears from my face
Hide the fear that leaves no trace
Don't hit me mummy
Don't hit me anymore
You never heard the silent screams
Only the nightmares and never the dreams
Please don't hit me mummy
Don't hit me anymore.

She slammed the door shut and her footsteps thudded into the distance. Checking the marks on my hands I climbed crying and trembling into bed. I curled up like a foetus and tried to stop myself from shaking and from the uncontrollable crying. Eventually I would fall asleep.

I found it very difficult to be a part of this new family and to feel loved, I felt I had to try harder, be nicer, offer more kindness, be something I didn't want to be or indeed knew how to be. Iit was like I had to become a chameleon and fit in to others peoples' mood swings while not allowed to have them myself.

I grew up in great fear of this woman and one day after yet another painful beating I found the courage to ask,

'Why she did you bother to adopt me?' (Which I can tell you

was a very brave thing to do, to answer back or give her lip). To this day the answer still resonates through my head.

'We adopted you as we wanted a non-white child,' she replied with all the love and kindness of the plague.

I stood in stunned silence as my body ached from yet another beating and just heartbroken at her cold callous remarks which cut like a serrated knife. I had hoped she would have said that, 'You were beautiful' or that 'You had lovely eyes' or even that they just 'loved me'. To hear that I was just a colour and little else made my life and my-self-esteem fall like autumn leaves from a tree and I began to hate myself.

My Father. or for that matter any other members of the family, did nothing to protect me nor did my Father show any real feelings or emotions. Both my parents were emotionally very cold. There was very little hugging in this house. My Father worked in insurance in the City of London and would commute every day to Aldgate; he always left the house with a kiss for Mother and a peck on the head for the other siblings. Most of the time he would forget to kiss me - soon, he forgot altogether and again I was plunged into self-doubt, asking myself, 'why had he forgotten to kiss me again?'

Life was very strict with lots of rules which I found a bit hard. I found it very hard to belong as there was little or no physical contact except for the beatings. If I didn't do exactly what I was told when I was told, then life became quite unpleasant. For instance, if I hadn't finished or refused to eat all the food on my plate, it would be served cold for breakfast the next morning. Forcing me to do something I just wouldn't do began, I believe, the onset of my failure to be as good as their own children. I felt that I was already a disappointment to them all. It didn't help either when I was out shopping with her and strangers would stare and sometimes ask, 'What's that?'

'Oh, it's adopted, it's an orphan,' my mother would sometimes reply.

Every Sunday we would all be marched off to the Quaker Meeting House in Rayners Lane, where I would be separated from my family and put in with other children and fed crap about being a sinner and that some innocent man died on a cross because of my selfish sins. Everywhere I looked I seemed to be at fault and blamed. I hated all this, but through fear I just accepted that I was indeed the son from hell's armpit.

One day my brother and I were arguing while sitting in the family Dormobile in the car park of the Quaker Meeting House, and he punched me full in the mouth, splitting my bottom lip wide open. That didn't help me, my-self-esteem or fears ; nor was being offered sixpence from my Grandmother to basically, 'shut the fuck up.'

When I was old enough, I was allowed to join the adults on a wooden bench where I would pray for forgiveness to the floor. I didn't really understand religion and the teachings about me being a 'sinner' which really got to me and made me quite fearful – yeah, like I needed to be in more fear! So now religion, my Mother, my Headmaster, the bullies at my school and now, even my brother, all gave me reasons to be scared, and I was. (Mind you, I have never seen a Quaker carry a gun, knife and machete, cut someone's head off, rape an altar boy or kill anyone - they seem to have some parts of religion spot on).

Dustbin Lid…

Since I was a dustbin lid
I've been beaten like a dog
Called a thousand insults
Oh, did I mention wog?
Since I was a dustbin lid
Abused in my children's home
Left in pain and isolation
And learnt how to be alone
Since I was a dustbin lid.

CHAPTER THREE
MY VERY FIRST CHRISTMAS

My first Christmas arrived with my mother creeping into my bedroom and placing an old knee length sock to the bottom of my bed, (oh yes I was wide awake, just from pure pajama- wetting excitement, but couldn't let on). After she left, I slipped out of my bed to inspect this weird gift. I opened the sock to find a walnut, 'Mmmmm,' I thought, 'what a totally crap mean chap Father Christmas was even though he was a transvestite and dressed up as my mum.'

I explored deeper into the magic sock, 'Oh a tangerine, whoopee,' a slight improvement on a rock hard walnut that I couldn't crack open, but then I found chocolate. 'Oh yes, now we're talking', I whispered while quickly demolishing it, but then hesitating to think, 'Oh perhaps I wasn't supposed to do that'. So hastily and in fear, I put all the goods and walnut back into the sock and then placed it back under the mattress and pretended that I had never ever seen it before in my life when I was woken up at 7 a.m.

I ran around with the sugar rush inspecting the Christmas tree and all the shiny boxes, sneakily trying to see how many had my name on them.

Soon excitement filled the air and the front door bell rang and rang as stranger after stranger arrived bearing more and more gifts. These people I was told were my Uncles and Aunts and their children, and I think I may well have been introduced but being shy beyond belief, I probably hid. There was a general buzz around the normally quiet and almost controlled home with lots of people speaking, and all of it I couldn't understand.

We all sat down to dinner; there must have been over twenty adults but no children of my age, which I found a bit hard. Eyes looked me up and down while we all sat around the dining table gorging ourselves fat with food. The strangers kept staring at me. I felt embarrassed, so I slipped silently under the table where I stayed looking at the mass of legs and stockings, where I felt safe.

Soon it was present-giving time so we all piled into the sitting room and presents were passed around. One of the uncles - I think it was Syd - took charge of the giving.

'To Margo with love from Uncle Harry and Dot', he would say in his deep, gravelly, ex-army, chain smoking voice, 'Oh is that for me?' Mother would reply in mock surprise as she carefully removed the paper and utter, 'Oh this paper is so beautiful, such a shame to ruin it', she would whine.

'Oh for God's sake, just open the present,' I thought, trapped in a little world I just didn't understand.

Boredom soon ensued until I heard those magic words,

'To Kim with much love from blablabla'

I carefully ripped the wrapping paper off and pulled out present after present, colouring books and toys. One toy almost made me pass out with excitement and to be honest I have no idea who bought this gift for me but was met with...

'Oh you're far too generous, we don't want to spoil it, do we?' Mother would say in her best posh accent.

'Oh yes we do, spoil me something rotten,' I whispered under my breath as I pulled out a battery-operated robot with flashing lights. I was made to stand and say 'thank you' Uncle and Auntie or Grandmother or brother or sister, I always found that a tad difficult, but with my new toys, I was off and upstairs playing alone with my new best friends.

Soon the dinner gong was bashed and again we all piled back into the dining room for yet more food and again I found myself listening to words and conversations I just didn't understand. Soon I did begin to have a strange fascination for these words and, of course, stocking clad legs.

My bedtime of 7 p.m. soon arrived and I was told to go and change into my pajamas and dressing gown, then come downstairs to say goodnight. I then returned to my pit, ladened with fat stomach and gifts. I unhappily got into bed whining.

I couldn't sleep for the noise and then the music and the acrid smell of tobacco as it hung off my clothes and around the house.

Talking of music, this house resounded with either absolute silence or music coming from everywhere, except from me. All my siblings played instruments, which included cello, double base, violin, viola, piano and guitar, and I believe all went to the Royal Academy of Music, which is situated on the Marylebone Road. My brother Jonathan had his own band called the Method which included Jake Riviera. Some might ask 'Well who the hell is Jake Riviera?' Well only the founder of Stiff Records, and both my brothers went to school with a certain Reg Dwight. Personally, I think both were better pianists and all round musicians. Apparently, Jonathan was given the chance to play in a band with Ronnie Wood. I must admit to being a bit star struck with both my brothers' and sisters' musical abilities, and the longish hair and general Beatles/Rolling Stones look about them. I had no musical abilities, except I could sing. I was made to sing in front of my class in my first week at Headstone School.

When there was no playing of instruments in the house, we listened mostly to classical music. The radio was usually on somewhere, and having three older teenage siblings meant hearing loads of great music - and, believe me, there was some brilliant music then.

Most evenings each sibling was safely in the confines of their own bedroom and then the cacophony began. Sometimes the music was relaxing and a joy to listen to, but other times not. I was given a few piano lessons by my mother (she was a music teacher) but I just couldn't get it. I couldn't make beautiful sounds and my impatience, temper tantrums and the fact that I was being sent away to boarding school didn't help.

The next day was similar to the Christmas day with lots of eating, lots of me hiding, inhaling smoke and listening to conversations that I could never join in. We didn't have a television then so, guitars and piano at the ready, we sang songs, which again were a bit rubbish as I had no idea of the words. One was 'Michael rowed the boat ashore, hallelujah', which I felt wasn't really worthy of a hallelujah. I mean, rowing a boat, 'Michael had a fish on his head or Michael saved the human race,' now that would be worthy of a hallelujah. Seems I found cynicism and sarcasm at a very early age. Well I thought it was funny, but that's because no one really spoke with me, just at me.

All too soon Christmas activities would end and I remember getting really upset, and not just because of the end to the excitement and jovial attitude. (I was never hit at Christmas time). Soon the house returned to the normal pace and I just played with my toys and carried on feeling alone.

CHAPTER FOUR
PAIN

One bored day, I watched as my Mother did the ironing. She left the room, the hot iron, and me to get more washing in from the garden. I inquisitively and stupidly pressed my left hand hard on to the hot iron. I screamed and screamed, as the pain was unbelievable. I pulled the melting flesh and burning hand from the iron. Soon she rushed in to find me in a state of blind panic and, if that wasn't bad enough, then made me put my burnt hand under cold water. This didn't really endear me to her, but I soon caught on that pain equals attention.

I continued to do all manner of painful things to myself. For instance, I had a sheriff's badge with a two inch pin attached to the back. I was walking bare foot in my brother's bedroom where the badge was left on the floor, pin sticking upright at ninety degrees, and guess what cretin trod on it? I felt the sharp razor sharp needle as it scythed its way into the heel of my foot. I fell on to the bed trying not to squeal in pain. Gently I pulled it out and the odd thing was, it didn't hurt; perhaps I was beginning to master pain.

In the back garden there was a dogleg in the path and while I was learning to ride my bike, I would often wobble uncontrollably around this area, which resulted in me falling off into the rose bushes. When you only have shorts and tee shirt on, there is little protection from the thorns. I would constantly fall into the rose bushes, cutting and slicing my bare arms and legs, and then be unable to move without extreme pain. I would shout out for help and wait to be saved, normally by an irate Mother. Time and time again I would fall into the roses, but for some strange reason I didn't take a detour across the lawn, (perhaps that was because that was a punishable offence). If it was a choice of thorns or a telling off, I chose thorns because not only did I get attention, but I also go a little bit of sympathy. More often than not, I got just a telling off. It was almost as if my fear of falling actually made me fall off. So I would gladly harm myself at school or at home because I realised: *this* equates to receiving attention. I was in great need of that.

Once while at school, after scoring a goal in the playground, I ran off to celebrate by sliding across the asphalt, ripping all the skin from my knees. I got a right bollocking for this act of stupidity, but I also got the attention I searched for. Then I spent the next month pulling off the scabs, so my fearlessness grew and I felt invincible - but also, very scabby.

Chapter Five
School

My very first memory of my new infant and junior school was actually before term had started, when I was taken for the short walk down the road to 'see how I liked it', as if I had any choice in the matter. For some reason I was taken at lunch time and made to walk with my mother through a deathly quiet dining room where I felt that every single child had stopped eating, talking and playing to stare at the child being forcefully dragged through the quiet stillness of a silent dining hall. I was made to 'sit' and in a loud overbearing voice she boomed, 'Would you like some lovely ice cream and jelly? Oh ice cream and jelly, that's your favourite isn't it, isn't it?'

I wanted to hide under the table, but there was little chance of escaping since all the other kids kept staring at me. I threw a massive moody sulk.

'Na, I don't want it,' I yelled in my rough uneducated London accent.

I knew instinctively that wasn't the correct response. I'm pretty sure she would have been alot happier if I had said,

'Oh what joy and happy tiding ma-ma, I am so very grateful for the kindness bestowed on my urchin-type head that I will forever be in your debt and servitude.'

One thing that I found hard to understand, apart from the punishment, was a language she would often use while speaking about me, even when I was sat in front of the family or listening from behind a closed door. This language I think was called Agy-Bagy…where she would add the letters a, g and y to the end of each word. For instance, I would now be 'heagy isagy aagy odiousagy littleagy shitagy.'

I never once caught on to what it meant, and it was only recently explained to me. I thought it was a language called Esperanto. Sadly all this did was pour more unhappiness on to my already sinking heart.

I also had a pretty torrid time at school because of name calling, which seemed to start from day one. It hurt, not just because of the words, but because it made me feel different to the other kids and all I really wanted to do was to fit in and be liked. Also there were many uncomplimentary comments about 'having no parents, being an orphan, and being adopted', but the name I remember being called and hated the most was 'wog'. My schoolmates and I tried to work out what this meant and the closest we got was 'western oriental gentleman.' There was one day at lunchtime when it seemed the entire school was walking around with arms linked repeating, 'Christine Keeler loves Kim Wheeler.' The word wog seemed to follow me around like a lost puppy until I left this school and also my next two. When I had left school and ventured forth into the big bad world, the name calling changed, and I was promoted to 'Paki'… well, 'fucking Paki,' actually.

My brother, once noticing my tears, asked what the matter was.

'The name calling at school, I'm not a wog, am I Jonathan?' I whined.

'No one is going to call my brother a wog,' he vehemently replied.

Did I feel proud of him, or did I feel proud of him? At last, someone is actually taking notice of my feelings.

But this conversation was sadly overheard by Mother, who dismissed the entire story as 'make believe and even if they did say these things you shouldn't worry about them.' Well I did.

Sadly, the abuses didn't stop.

Fallen...

I feel that I'm dead already
But not yet fallen down
I'm sure I'll spend more painful times
With my face flat to the ground
So every day I stand alone
Praying for help from above
Reaching the same old conclusions
That all I need is love
But can you ever love this child
Whose jigsaw's fallen to bits
Help the boy pick up the pieces
And somehow make them fit
I wouldn't know what love is
If it came knocking at my door
Doesn't feel like I've had my share
But really I would love some more
Understand me inside
You will see I'm not so bad
Trying desperately to free myself
From a childhood you never had.

CHAPTER SIX
THIEF

I started to steal at school. Nobody enticed me to do it; I just did it and the school caretaker was my target. He had a little room next to the stairs, which was full of the kinds of goodies I had no interest in at all. What he did have, and what I wanted and stole, was his collection of 'football cards'. It's what all the other kids collected, and because I had no money, I couldn't afford to buy the gum to collect the cards. 'Why buy the gum when I can steal the cards?' It was dead easy, and I never got caught.

Soon I was stealing from shops and even did it when I went shopping with my Mother. Nobody would suspect an innocent child. When I went to the shops on my own I would steal anything from toys to cigarette holders, ties and hankies, any old shit; I just wanted something, anything, just for me. Most of my thieving days were from Soper's in Harrow. I didn't, however, steal from my family as I was already blamed for everything and anything. Having older siblings who would readily grass me up even when I had done no wrong would just exacerbate the already fraught situation. I wasn't that thick. This continued even when we went abroad on holiday. Stealing chocolate was my favorite, and as I stole more, the cockier I got. I even went into a men's clothing shop in Spain by myself, walked up to the tie rack, picked out the most colourful tie, stuck it in my pocket, and cheerily walked out, saying goodbye in Spanish - or it might well have been 'I am a cheese plant'.

The staff just grinned back, not knowing that I had a nice red tie in my pocket. When the tie was produced some days later, I just innocently said that I had 'found it'. I knew my Mother didn't believe me, but without my being caught red-handed, she couldn't prove anything. That soon changed. After another trip to Sopers in Harrow, I was rumbled after trying to hide my hoard of stuff under my bed. I got the rhythmic slaps across bare legs while being berated in perfect timing with the slaps. A few minutes later, Mother marched me to the car and drove me to Sopers. We walked through the back entrance to the security office where I was made to hand over all my ill-gotten gains and apologise, while my Mother gave me a right bollocking in front of what seemed like the entire staff. This, however, did not stop me thieving. In fact, it just made me worse, and I would steal anything and was clever enough not to get caught. The lowest point for me was when I stole a church collection box. That night, after counting the pennies, I lay awake in bed feeling guilty. I didn't return the money but neither did I steal money again. Perhaps the fear of an unforgiving, cruel God got to me, or perhaps I was learning right from wrong - and it was about bloody time, what a little shit I'd been!

I still don't know why or how this all started - perhaps I was just trying to fight back at the injustices bestowed upon me, or perhaps I was just getting a thrill not giving a monkey's if I got caught. The beatings didn't bother me anymore as I had got used to the pain.

However, my thieving habits did change when I was sent to boarding school as I wouldn't steal from those around me. But when summer holidays came around, I was often sent away to adventure camps. I would team up with other kids or go solo to steal money from the other tents. I showed not a shred of guilt.

CHAPTER SEVEN
NIGHTMARES

Throughout my young childhood, I had horrendous nightmares which would always result in my waking up screaming uncontrollably whilst pissing the entire contents of my bladder into my bed. I had nightmares about being chased through leafy lanes by an alien-type figure, (the head resembled a horse's skull but the body was of human form). I was always able to keep away from it as it chased me for what seemed like miles and miles and miles of leafy country lanes. I then came across a small building where I rushed through the front doors and eventually found a place to hide in a cupboard, peering breathlessly through the gap in the shut doors. The beast entered the room and searched menacingly for its prey, grunting and snarling. Suddenly, it turned round and stared right at where I was hiding, sweating profusely and shaking behind the flimsy doors of my protective cupboard. It suddenly charged, closer and closer towards me, and ripped open the doors. Then in absolute terror, I would wake up screaming and pissing gallons into my bed.

Another nightmare was… I was drifting slowly upward from my bed to the ceiling and floating around, unable to stop or change direction. I slowly floated towards a metal grate. I desperately tried to stop myself, but the more I struggled, the closer I got to the dark black grill. I got closer and closer until I was directly below it. It was dark and there was a stench of cold death about it. Then suddenly, the face of an ugly, haggard woman would appear inches from my face screaming at me. I couldn't move. I was inches away from this repulsive hag-ridden face with its repugnant breath and death in her insane eyes. I again woke screaming, punching thin air and pissing buckets into the bed.

Yet another nightmare was… being on a sunny peaceful beach while looking out over the calm sea, when all of a sudden the placid light blue waters began to change to choppy darker waters, and then turn to a grey, menacing swell. The skies darkened to moody and fierce. Suddenly the sea turned a deathly black and rose up one hundred feet into the air, towering over me. I tried to run but I was rooted to the spot. Then it came crashing down towards me, and as hard as I tried, I could not get away from it. It felt as real as if I was actually there. I could even taste the salt water. Again I woke up screaming and soaking wet with piss.

OK, just one more then…but this wasn't a nightmare. It was more like a journey, but quite a journey. I was standing in a space ship (I would like to add that this was before I had seen a television, or knew about space or space travel, or indeed space ships) looking out of a very large oval port hole at a blue-ish object in the distance. I asked while pointing at the object,

'What's that?'

'Your new home,' was the soft reply,

'Will I be alone?' I asked without too much concern with 'the new home' bit.

'Yes, but we will always be with you.'

Weird or what?

Oh what fun I was having - nightmares at night and fearful

of almost everything during the day! The nightmares and bed-wetting continued for five years, and I was always admonished that this was a sign of weakness. I retreated totally into myself, lying on my bed scratching the plaster off the walls of my cell until my fingers bled. Because I was constantly picked on and called names at school, I used to scrub my skin with Ajax cleanser, hoping in a vain attempt to remove my colour. This worked as my skin was now red raw, just like my emotions.

I was then informed that I was being 'sent away' to a boarding school, This came directly after another bruising encounter with Mrs. Gnarled Hands and I guess that was when I realized that I just wasn't wanted, or that's how it felt at the time. What was odd about this very last physical beating was that I didn't feel any pain. I clearly remember turning to look at her without fear and staring into her angry eyes, probably with resignation, or perhaps I was just so used to the pain that it didn't bother me anymore. It was the way she looked back at me as I stared at her. She almost look frightened and I remember thinking, 'You know, I'm getting bigger every day, and one day I could easily and might even, snap you in two.'

I felt unloved, I hated my life, hated myself and I hated my mother.

I guess I was about eight. I still kept wetting the bed and the horrendous nightmares continued, until I was packed off to boarding school. There was no way that I could wet the bed as I would have been bullied and ridiculed for such immature and childish behavior, and not forgetting that we were all taught,

'We don't do emotions and we don't do pain'.

Chapter Eight
Boarding school awaits

Before I ventured off to the great unknown called boarding school, I was sent to the local school with the wonderful name of Headstone! I duly arrived on my first day in shorts, the only child to attend senior big boys' school in shorts. That went over really well because I wasn't ridiculed or laughed at that much - only for about the entire term! Then the verbal abuses began and again it was the original and cunningly witty Wog, which by now I had learned to ignore. I hated this place, hated everything about it.

All too soon the day came when I was ready to be packed off. Again the emotions of the day got to me as I was reminded of the exact same emotions I had experienced when being dragged kicking and screaming from my children's home. This time though, I wasn't kicking or screaming, well not out loud, but inside there was unbridled turmoil, hurt, anger, rejection, loneliness and a great fear of the unknown. What would have made this transition a bit easier to bear would have been a loving send off. Sadly, there was none. There were no emotional goodbyes from my family; in fact the house was empty apart from a nervous kid and a hurried mother.

I put on my new school uniform, which clashed against my newly acquired sun tan. I was bricking myself, dreading the possible extent of colour prejudice I was about to meet. I was also reassuringly told that this school 'didn't believe in corporal punishment'.

'Oh what joy, what a relief,' so as you can imagine, that cheered me up... until I received, yes, you guessed it, corporal punishment at a Quaker Boarding School.

While we drove the sixty plus miles in absolute silence, I reflected on what was looming around the last bend, just hoping that I would have a heart attack or be involved in a car crash, anything but be sent away. Soon we rolled into the grounds of my new school, my home for the next four plus years.

We were met by my new housemaster Mr. Francis, a bald middle-aged man, quite friendly at first, who then spoke for a few minutes to my Mother as I looked nervously around my new surroundings. Suddenly a wave, or was it relief, washed over me, 'Ah ha, no more beatings; no more forced fed food left cold for breakfast; no more Agy Bagy; no more Kimagy havingagy aagy massiveagy sulkagy; no more hurt; no more hiding in the attic; no more bed wetting; no more scratching the walls in sadness, anger and frustration; no more bleeding fingers—and, just perhaps, no more fearsome nightmares. Suddenly I was snapped out of my dream state as she turned to me and said quite abruptly, 'Well, goodbye then,' and walked away.

I suddenly felt very alone standing next to the grinning, bald housemaster. He then showed me to my dorm and pointed to my bed. There was another kid lying on his bed reading the Beano. I nodded hello, put my stuff away, jumped on to my bed where my new cell mate Andrew Arnold (who became a pilot in the RAF) gave me one of his comics. I felt at ease, and I must admit to feeling an immense sense of relief. 'Well, at least she can't hit me or hurt me anymore,' I thought.

I stopped the bed-wetting instantly and the nightmares slowly disappeared, but the abuse about the colour of my skin, my origins, name and my parentage continued.

As I mentioned before, this was a Quaker Boarding School where I was told there would be 'no corporal punishment'. Sadly, this proved to be untrue as I was often slippered in front of the class, and had a blackboard cleaner thrown at my head from a full twenty feet, which cut it open. I still carry that scar. I got accused of doing things I just couldn't possibly have done. Again, I began to feel that I was being unfairly and systematically hammered at every chance by some of the overbearing bullying teachers.

My hatred towards institutionalization grew and so too did my already volatile anger.

I soon settled down and began to make friends, but the schooling was extremely strict. We had prep every evening for two hours and even had lessons on Saturday mornings, but we did get Wednesday and Saturday afternoons off. Sunday was a free day except for going to the meeting house to pray and break wind, the noisier the better, but sadly the longer the detention.

There was only one occasion when I became homesick and thought about running away, but I wouldn't have got far because the school had a mascot which was a hungry cheetah.

I began to excel in some sports ,but truthfully it was just my escape as I was pretty crappy at all my other subjects. With sports my fitness levels rocketed. We had five-mile, cross-country runs in winter and also played rugby in winter. As the school was on a hill in the middle of nowhere, it was also bloody freezing and there were no warm track suits to wear. If we were lucky we could cover ourselves in whale blubber. I was crap at rugby, but man could I run, so I was put on the wing and actually began to enjoy the physical brutality of this sport.

I was also hopeless at football, but I did try. No one can ever say that I didn't try or I lacked bottle. I was soon promoted to goal keeper and played for the juniors and was suddenly thrust, (due to the senior goalkeeper's severe bouts of illness caused by diphtheria or perhaps rabies) to the senior football team. The bus waited as I busied myself trying to get my kit. I could hear the abuse already. I tentatively walked onto the stinking, old, pewk-making, bone-shaking bus as I felt the piercing eyes of all these grown men staring at me. Nervous? Oh yes, just a tad.

I had two games in two weeks. We lost both 10-0 - yes 10-0 - and again I was demoted to 'fuck off Wheeler', which funnily enough was also my name in rugby! While playing football on the right wing for my house, I was met with a chorus of 'woggy wheeler on the wing' with my size nine leather, steel toe-capped, World War II hand-me-downs. My already insecure self-belief dissipated at some considerable speed, to the point where I was relieved not to be picked to play on a team.

I taught myself table tennis and tennis - how safe was that - and I became very good at both of these sports. In fact, I spent all my spare time every evening improving and honing my skills, bashing away like I was demented. Eventually, I was in the finals of an inter-school table tennis competition. The game was set in the other boy's house as he had won the toss. I walked into a crowded common room, kids everywhere. I wished I had played the game in my house's common room as I think home advantage would have helped cure my nerves. I started well, then my game fell to bits and I lost to a boy called

Bishop, who only had one finger and one thumb. I think I lost on purpose, perhaps out of pity for Bishop, or perhaps he was just better with two fingers than I was with all mine. He was the hero of the day and I was sadly demoted back to 'fuck off Wheeler,' but, to be honest, in my own little private world, I was just happy taking part.

It was lucky that I was quite good in sports because I really was quite hopeless in almost everything else, except maybe English literature.

I even managed to get one out of a hundred in a geography exam as I preferred to just gaze out of the window and, all too often, ending up in detention and paying visits to the headmaster.

The weekend evenings were spent either watching some really appalling films or at the school disco, where I had the dancing skills of an amoeba. The boys danced in large circles while holding pretend guitars, and the girls danced in another part of the hall. There was definitely no fraternizing with them as there was always a teacher on hand to pour cold water onto any amorous erections. Our only cure for inappropriate erections and the onset of puberty was that we polished ourselves silly in our dorms at night. We called this practice, 'Lights out, tents up' and, if I remember correctly, I was particularly good at it.

I mentioned earlier about my love for music, and it continued throughout my boarding school years. Owning a radio was the coolest thing and at every opportunity someone would be playing one somewhere. I still believe 1967 was the finest year for music ever, and I think it was that year that a certain guitarist changed my life and views of music forever.

When I first heard the opening salvo to Purple Haze, I thought 'What the hell was that?' My brother bought me my very first single (45's) which was Jimi Hendrix's 'All Along the Watchtower' and suddenly Wheeler became a cooler kid. The list of great music is almost endless and it was listening to music that saved my sad life in my sad shell in my horrible, sad, lonely state while bad times were occurring at boarding school. Listening to music is still where I go when I'm in that bad place.

An opportunity arose when we were given the chance to go horse riding, and, as I seemed useless at sports that involved a team, I thought, 'Well one horse and one rider sounds perfect.' So a hurried, groveling letter was sent home begging that I be allowed this escape from the boredom of school. Of course, I promised my parents to do anything they asked of me (I learned from a very early age the adept skills of lying through my teeth.) Soon I got a reply and the answer was Yes. I was chuffed, if not somewhat surprised.

I think twelve of us eventually got the call up and were soon whisked off to the local horse riding stables. Suddenly, I found myself sitting on the back of a fat farting Thelwell pony, as wide as it was high. Another kid got the best horse, a seventeen-hands beauty that knew instinctively what she was supposed to do. Mine, however, was fat, hopeless and continually farted, which reduced me to hysterics, much to the anger of instructors. But having the fat, hopeless, farting cretin nag made me work that much harder, and when we had an end of term gymkhana, I actually managed to come in second, which in my eyes was a great result.

With horse-riding, table tennis, tennis, and being pretty good at most sports that didn't involve teams, I had found a kind of happiness in my life and even a self-belief which was lacking in all my other school activities. I just hoped that when I left school my parents would afford me the gift of continuing my love for and my self-belief in sport. After all, the other kids were all to be sent to university and I instinctively knew I wouldn't be doing that. I was out of luck and there was to be no more sport and no university – think I was just a tad too thick.

It took me a while to stop the feelings of being not good enough and not as good as the other clever siblings. OK, I admit to being useless academically, but I was very good and very proud of the sports I chose. I know that I could have achieved a lot more doing something I felt good at, which helped me build my self-confidence. Sadly, that dream was smashed, as you will see later on.

Boarding school was harsh; rules were almost military, and haircuts were definitely worse than military. They were carried out by the local farmer using blunt scissors and savage hands and with absolutely no idea of style, gentleness or art. A pudding basin haircut was what you got laddy and you should be fucking grateful.

The school was filled by a real assortment of kids and finding which group to join was difficult for me. There were the sporty types; you know, the ones with all the hair, sideburns, gravely voices, and most annoyingly, the pubes. Then there were the day boys, who were allowed home every night as they were local. There were also the Witney boys, three of whom were in my dorm. There the silent types, who didn't feel attached to anyone.. Then there was me and perhaps a couple of other kids like the first one I was introduced to when I first walked into my new dorm, someone whom everyone seemed to hate. So I latched onto him as I felt sorry for him. On my second day some older man-boy ran over and hit him full on the nose, and for no apparent reason. I remember thinking, 'Mmmmm Quakers are so gentle and peaceful aren't they?' I learned in time that there were many among us who weren't Quakers at all. They were just told, like myself to attend Quaker school because our parents were practicing Quakers. Most of us couldn't really give a toss, and I certainly didn't.

Some holidays I went home and some I went to adventure camps in Wales, alone. I was OK with this as I had been sent away on holidays since I first joined the cubs, the scouts and then went with the Quakers to Quaker camp. All were run to a military precision! The army would have been proud: bed, kit and clothes were all brought out of the tent and laid out immaculately to be inspected daily. I soon cottoned on to the fact that each tent was marked on a daily basis and the scores were written in pencil and hung just outside our tents. So with rubber and pencil in hand, I changed our scores and no one was any the wiser.

After the initial dread, I soon mucked in and again I found I was good at most things I was told to do. Canoeing was one, but climbing mountains…well not so much mountains, but they seemed like mountains at the time. Pot holing made me shit myself. Orienteering was good fun. Pony trekking I was a master at, almost a natural. I could see a profession for me in the army after I left the safety and confines of school. But if I found the discipline hard to swallow at boarding school, how could I ever survive the British Army?

Some holidays, as I said, I went home. On one occasion just my eldest brother and my Mother went to France for two weeks. I didn't speak to her once and nor did she speak to me the whole time I was home. The physical beatings may have stopped, but that was now replaced by mental abuse and often I would actually looked forward to going back to school.

My favorite holiday though was when school friend John Park from Birkenhead and I cycled all around Devon and Somerset. We met at Bristol train station, bikes safe and locked, and travelled in the luggage coach. I was particularly proud of my racing bike because I had to work an entire school holiday and do several odds jobs to save the £17 as my parents wouldn't buy it for me. It had the latest super-duper gear change switch at the end of the aluminum drop handlebars; ten speed; double clanger with sexy, polished, chrome mud guards, which were crap in the rain, but hey I didn't care.

So, ready and excited, we met and began our fourteen-day adventure cycling from one youth hostel to the next. I actually cycled up Cheddar Gorge, (big deal, I hear you shout; well it bloody well was to us since those bikes and panniers weighed a bloody ton). Coming down again was almost suicidal and for a frightened few moments, I thought Park had died as he tore off down the road at full speed and even I couldn't catch up. Suddenly I heard an angry coach horn blare, the hissing sound of air brakes and the stench of rubber burning. To my horror I thought Park was dead, crushed under the wheels of a happy camper's coach party, when in fact he was laughing his silly bollocks off in a lay by.

We had absolute freedom and, when you compare this to the rare freedom of boarding school, you can understand why we both thoroughly enjoyed it. It wasn't quite 'five go mad in Dorset' but not far off target, with lashings of ginger beer and cooking our own food and occasionally sleeping under the stars. It seemed most of my happy memories only came when I was as far away as possible from my Mother.

I was growing up but I was also turning into a bit of a bully. I wonder why.

One day, and now a respected fifth former with special fifth form jacket, I walked into the bogs to find three juniors trying to drown a first form kid by hanging him upside down by his feet and dangling his head down the bog. Did I run and help the kid? Did I, like hell! I walked over grabbed the boy's feet, ordered 'flush' and watched with glee and almost maniacal laughter as this poor kid got a thorough drenching as I ran out giggling. So whoever you were kid, I apologise profusely.

One evening all us male seniors were packed off to a school in Banbury to get a slim and quite hopeless idea of what sort of work we would like to achieve when we left the confines of school. We all meandered in and around the perimeter of the school hall were all kinds of people sitting behind desks giving out information. I stood silently and thought, 'There's not much choice and none that include sports', but there was an army recruiter there. I sidled up to the vacant chair and sat down, perhaps not the wisest of moves.

'Yes,' this booming voice appeared from under a peaked cap, eyes so sharp they scythed holes into my face.

'I'm sort of interested in joining the Army when I leave school,' I wailed in my still silly high-pitched voice.

'Do you laddy?'

'Yes, well I'm good at sports' and then I realised, 'but sod all else' I whispered under my breath.

'So you want to join the Army do you laddy?'

'This is going to be a very long drawn out pointless conversation' I thought to myself, 'I'm having a conversation with a retard in red cap.'

'No not really,' I replied and stood up scraping the chair across the highly polished floor.

I walked aimlessly about for the next hour while the repetitive retard scything eyes tore at my pristine flesh.

I hid.

Well that was a total waste of my time. I asked the other kids if they had any better luck. 'About the same as you Wheeler,' came the pissed off replies.

All too soon it was time to leave my third and quite probably my happiest home. Saying the tearful goodbyes to all the great friends I had made over the past four years and to the many girls I had snogged was almost heartbreaking. I just didn't want to go home and I didn't want to lose these friends who had become extremely important to me. In spite of all the name calling, I knew I would miss them terribly. I didn't want to go home as I still feared what lay ahead.

I had matured and become something that I was really quite proud of. Although I say I was a tad thick, as far as I can remember I left school with no certificates of secondary education. I had learned canoeing, sailing, horse-riding, pony trekking, abseiling, potholing, cycling, football, rugby, table tennis, tennis, and athletics, all of which I wrongly thought was a result to be proud of. Sadly, my parents didn't agree. I left this happy-ish place with all its ups and downs and returned home on the train from Banbury Station, aged fifteen years and ten months, and alone.

Chapter Nine
Home alone

I moved back home, which was now totally devoid of siblings. Suddenly, as I was thrust into absolute loneliness, it dawned on me that I now faced the big bad world alone. I was allowed a month's holiday, which I spent by myself as all my friends from junior school had all moved on. I went to the cinema alone, went cycling alone, and went shopping alone.

Then I had to find a job. I thought about the angry army retard and decided to give it another shot. Unbeknown to my parents, I went to the local Army Recruiting Office and was pleasantly surprised at my welcome and the fact there was no wall-eyed Scotsman with laser beam eyes. I filled in forms and more forms.

'Are you sure you're sixteen sonny? The smart-as-a-university-graduate sharp uniform enquired.

'Erm well not quite, in a month's time I am Sir'.

'Well we will have to write to your parents for their permission'.

'Shit, I never thought of that'.

I was sent to a barracks in Kingsbury where the TA were stationed, just to have a look. To be honest it was all a tad overwhelming for me with lots of shouting and shiny shoes and sharp uniforms. I lined up with some other spotty youths and was stared at continually by all.

We were told what being a soldier in the British Army meant

and by the second sentence I had lost interest.

Some days later, an irate Mother stomped up the stairs, I'm guessing after they had received a letter from the MOD.

'No son of mine is ever going to join the Army,' she shouted,

'No son of mine is going to join the army, Sa,' I shouted back through the closed door. My humour was lost. Maybe another time, I promised myself; maybe another time when I didn't look twelve, my voice had broken, my balls had dropped and my eye-fighting skills were honed to perfection.

Well, after being sent for all kinds of shit jobs, I eventually got one, and it was the worst of the lot. It was as an apprentice gas fitter. So all my endeavors as a pretty fit sports-loving, mountain-climbing, Thelwell-pony-riding, rugby-playing, cross-country-running, pubescent oik were all for nothing, and I hated it. This job brought me back in contact with all the old prejudices that I thought I had left behind at school with children.

Sadly, racial and colour prejudice was rife.

I had taken an awful lot of crap at school and had learned how to defend myself, not just verbally but also with my fists. I knew they worked and I wasn't afraid to use them when I had had enough of the constant 'Woggy Wheeler syndrome'. Fighting wasn't really the answer to these anally retentive cretins, but I knew it was a good backup if all else failed. Here I was, surrounded by men, and nearly all of them did exactly what the kids for the past ten years had done.

So Monday morning came and, at 0745, I clocked in as an apprentice gas fitter and went directly to hell.

Chapter Ten
Losing my virginity/religion and job

I grew my hair long, began to smoke cigarettes, and (although I had tried to look cool at school smoking, and failed) tried dope but just threw up, hated my job, hated my life at home but did get my first girlfriend. When I say first, I sort of had girlfriends at school, but this one was private and not shared around the boarding school and was all mine. Her name was Heather. She was blond, intelligent, sexy and what she saw in me is still a conundrum, and how we met even more perplexing. She was a virgin and so was I. I used to cycle to her home and have dinner with her parents and I felt accepted and liked by them as they were a far cry from the rigidity of life at my parents where I had to be home by the latest 9 p.m. - yes 9 p.m or be locked out. I was often locked out.

The abuses at work became intolerable and I fell out with almost everyone in charge and a lot of my co-workers. As I was just an apprentice, I just had to take all the shit they threw, and the worst bastard of them all was the area manager.

My skills at college were excellent. In my final practical exam where I had to plumb in a boiler, radiators and gas fire using all my newly-taught skills in copper, lead pipe and lead joints, I got top marks. I believe I got 99/100, and I was the proudest of them all, as I at last felt a sense of achievement. A few weeks later and a month or so before my final city and guilds exams, I was sacked, sacked for refusing to have my haircut and or wear a hair net by the thug colour-prejudiced area manager. I truly believe he just hated me as I didn't fit his criteria of a gas fitter.

I walked home and relayed the sad news to two extremely hacked-off parents who just got angry at me. There was no support, no lets all go and talk to the racist bastard who sacked me, nothing except anger. I was a failure, an absolute failure and where were all my siblings? At University and I was now down on the dole.

Not long after that I split up from Heather and I felt like crap. Someone passed me a joint; then someone passed me a thousand and I became lost. I lost self-belief, lost my drive. I even stopped playing guitar because every time I played I would be angrily told to 'turn that racket off'… but when the siblings played their musical instruments, however loudly or badly, not a negative word. So with having to sleep in the car on extremely cold nights as I refused to come home early, and with no job, no love or feelings of belonging ,I began to fall into the age-old trap of drugs, man!

I met other 'hairys' who played guitars, smoked dope, said 'man' a lot, giggled inanely for no reason, sat around listening to some great music, didn't work and seemed very content and happy. 'Well that will do for me,' I thought. I even began to sing and went to a recording studio in Pinner to record a record with some fellow hairys. Sadly the song was truly dreadful, it was called 'morning ride' and the first verse went, "Come on baby we're going for a morning ride, come on baby we've got to catch the morning tide". Truly dreadful, I couldn't sing that, but I did try, and after ten minutes of complete and utter embarrassment I said, 'no'. I think the truth was, I had no confidence and any knock would have made me crumble. The sound guy had asked me to 'ramp up the vocals'. I did try but felt insecure about being picked on, which I wasn't, I just felt I was.

The guy who played organ was called Roly Kerridge (who sadly passed away recently) and he ended up with a number one hit with the band Reflex with the song Politics of Dancing. One of the guitarists, called Ant Glynne, ended up playing on another number one record with Mike Oldfield's, Moonlight Shadow. He also went on to play with a whole host of musicians, including a tour with Rick Wakeman.

Why didn't I just ignore my parents' unhelpful negative words and just keep playing, why oh bloody why? That was one of my biggest regrets because music was in my blood. As I lost all my-self-confidence I just gave up and returned to smoking weed by the bucket and calling everyone man.

CHAPTER ELEVEN
HE'S LEAVING HOME

I couldn't wait to leave home. Imagine an eighteen year old having to be home by 10 p.m., and if I wasn't home I would have to sleep rough in the car. You may be pondering, 'Why on earth do you not have a front door key?' Well, I was never allowed a front door key. When I say never, I mean I *never ever* had the key to the front door, but at some point I was allowed a side door key.

So then started the onset of 'what to do with the rest of my life' that most angst filled teenagers have. To be honest, nothing really suited. The army was now a distant memory as smoking copious amounts of spliff dulled my get-up-and-go. Sadly my get-up-and-go had fallen asleep, and flying off to Planet Zanusi on a daily basis seemed a lot more fun. In truth, and with hindsight, it wasn't one of my best ideas and I should have stopped, but sadly I didn't. In fact, I smoked more and got to meet and participate in all manner of drugs and alcohol, mainly because all my friends and peers were. Don't forget I was locked away in one type of school prison or another during the sixties when drugs were rife and Peace and Love was the cool thing and not war. I felt that I was contributing to the peace movement by not killing.

I went from one dreadful dead end job to another - sowing mattresses, lathe turning, road sweeper, and night time petrol pump attendant to name a few. All were 'dead easy, don't have to use the brain, easy money, little future' kinds of jobs. Then I was offered a daytime petrol pump attendant's position just a few miles down the road. I went for the interview and sailed through it but was told, 'the hair has got to go.'

That night I cut off three years of growth and set about starting a new job and new life.

The job was easy but cold in the winter, with long hours, and tedious beyond belief, but there was a great group of guys who had no signs of prejudice, and for the first time I felt I belonged. The boss was a big, no-nonsense, tough guy who took absolutely no crap from anyone, had a fearsome reputation. Many feared him, though I did not as I had learned from an early age to keep my mouth shut, don't ask for anything (as many people saw the boss as a quick fix to the new television they had always wanted) and do my job. He was extremely generous and would often take us all out. Once we all went off to Wembley to watch boxing. The first fight I saw was John Conteh, who bashed his opponent into submission in the first round.

I loved the job and camaraderie but especially the cars. It was while I worked here that I got to take my driving test. I passed it first time, so many of the lads lost money betting against me. One thing you should never do is to say to me, 'You can't', because I will go out of my way and prove you wrong, and I still will.

So it was a great job, with a boss I trusted and respected and actually saw more as a father figure than my own father. He trusted me, and now with my brand new driving licence I was allowed to drive the cars. Tell me that an eighteen year old who looked twelve driving around in a brand new Rolls Royce wasn't cool - or the latest BMW, or Aston Martin! I had a shared flat a few miles down the road and life was great… except I still overdid the drink and drugs, which would ultimately be my downfall.

My ability to be up at 7 a.m. became an issue, and I would often arrive at work late and disheveled. It wouldn't be long until even the best boss I have ever had would tire of me, and soon he sacked me.

I again found myself at a loss, flitting from one rubbish job to another. Perhaps it was time to grow up. I eventually got myself a job as a truck driver and again the 'being on my own' seemed to fit perfectly with my character, happy to join in but also happy on my own. I was soon driving all over the country, and I loved the freedom with no boss looking over my shoulder. With my new-found happiness, time flew and I was eventually beginning to grow up.

CHAPTER TWELVE
IS THIS LOVE?

Well I eventually managed to reach twenty one and I spent my twenty-first birthday in St. Ives with a handful of close friends and many hairy hangers-on. I had a great job and what I believed to be a good, close group of friends, and life at that time was great. I did still suffer from depressions, and, sadly, they never gave me prior notice as to when they were about to strike. I couldn't understand the mood swings, nor could my friends. I found a part of me that I didn't understand or like, but while I smoked dope and drank copious amounts of alcohol, I would feel happy. Sadly, I didn't confront the emotions and background of my depressions and found running away far easier and a lot more fun than facing my past.

I met a lovely girl who refused point blank to let me have my lurid way. It was just what I wanted as prior to her, my girlfriends (except my very first one) were one night shags, sometimes two nights. On the whole, it was basically sleep and abandon. I thought any woman I slept with was obviously in love with me…how wrong was I?

I waited and waited for her to agree; twelve months soon elapsed and I was still not even allowed a quick grope. I began to look elsewhere, yes naughty Kim. Thankfully, I soon realised the stupidity of this immature choice and was soon back with her, but this did not guarantee anything more. She said she was falling in love with me and I felt I was also falling in love with her. It was a strange feeling but also one that brought new problems, with the most problematic being my insecurity showing itself as jealousy and mistrust. I trusted her; I didn't, however, trust men and from past experiences I wasn't wrong to do so. Close, so-called friends had already slept with my ex-girlfriends without a moment of guilt.

One day while on holiday in my brother's cottage in Morton hampstead, I asked her if she would marry me. Se said, 'Yes'. I was in absolute heaven and I just couldn't believe that she had agreed. But, sadly, deep inside, I felt that I just couldn't live up to her expectations or those of her father, whom I felt never really accepted me or even liked me. She came from a wealthy God-fearing family and I came from the gutter of society - and that's where the problem lay. I had so much self-doubt, self-loathing and weakness which I hadn't discussed with her for fear of rejection. I knew that this problem, along with my mood swings and jealousy, would determine not only our future but my future with all women. We never got married, and we have never spoken a word since we split up.

CHAPTER THIRTEEN
AUTHORITY BITES BACK

I still had enormous problems with authority; especially with the police whom I felt tended to pick on me. Either it was my long hair when I was a teenager or my off-white skin or indeed my snarling attitude towards being harassed. I was forever being pulled up and searched. To illustrate this, let's have another antidote.

I was walking home through North Harrow after buying some tennis balls which were in a plastic container with an aluminum sealed lid. I ambled home, and within a few yards of my street, I felt eyes staring at me. Sure enough, when I looked up three pairs of beady eyes were staring at me. Soon the sirens wailed and out jumped PC Pothole, who demanded to know my name, address and if I was a fighter/ boxer. I was politeness personified even though I felt a tad aggrieved to be pulled over yet again. Soon he was talking into his two-way radio when he turned to me and said those immortal words,

'You're fucking nicked'.

'Why?' I asked politely as my guts ran amok.

'Overdue fine,' the grinning plank replied and then added, 'of forty pounds'.

He then told me to put both my arms out, manacled my wrists, read the riot act and my rights (why are they called rights?) and arrested me. I was then placed into the back of his nice shiny car and told in no uncertain terms to put my hands on the seat in front and 'keep quite' as his colleague next to me eyeballed me menacingly.

We arrived at South Harrow Police Station where I was put into a cell and told that I would be there until Monday morning, when I'd be taken to court for trial and sentencing. Of course I went ballistic.

'Forty eight hours banged up for a fine, I'll pay the fine now!' I screamed through the closed and locked metal door.

No one was listening. I had to come up with a cunning plan. I noticed that they hadn't taken away my new box of tennis balls which, as I said earlier, was sealed with an aluminum lid.

'Ah ha,' I said to myself, grinning with the cunning of my cunning plan. I could see a way out of there, either by foot or by an ambulance. I pulled off the aluminum top, pulled up my shirt sleeves and slashed away at both my forearms.

The first twenty slashes didn't hurt, much; the last few did as I ran out of anger and adrenalin. I then hid the aluminum top and started to wipe the dripping blood around the cell walls whilst screaming my deranged head off. Within a few minutes the cell door was hurriedly opened and in walked another PC. He looked in disbelief at the new work of art on the walls and the carnage that was my arms and rushed out. Within a few more minutes he returned with a diminutive Asian Doc who sidled in stuttering under his breath, 'self-harm'.

I demanded to see somebody in authority as the cell door was left open and PC Pothole stood grunting on about strait jackets and beating me. Within ten minutes an ashen face appeared out of nowhere.

'My name is Superintendent Wheeler,' he said and made some wisecrack about having the same surname as me.

Unimpressed, I turned on my anger and raged at him, throwing all my toys out of my pram and giving him a right earful.

My arms were still bleeding but PC Pothole didn't even bother to give me any first aid. He just stood there grinning, looking at the pretty blood-stained walls. After about ten minutes of quite brutal sledging, PC Pothole and I were about to go toe to toe. With the mood I was in, I would have torn him to bits. Some minutes later the Superintendent reappeared and politely sneered.

'Mr Wheeler, you can go home as long as you pay the fine on Monday morning'.

'Ok, thank you very much. Now if you wouldn't mind, could you please let me out,' I said politely, and then screamed, 'of this fucking cell?'

I went to thank and shake the desk sergeant's hand.

'I'm not shaking hands with you, I don't what you've got,' he sneered.

Within what seemed minutes I had run a few miles towards home when a mate of mine saw me and gave me a lift home.

'Look at this,' I said as I rolled up my sleeves to show off the deep, still dripping-with-blood carnage. He recoiled in shock, and then took me home and rolled me a nice fat spliff. Soon I was grinning like a dead fox.

Monday morning duly arrived, as they often do, and I paid the overdue fine.

A week later, there was an incident reported in the Harrow Observer about a man who had been beaten up in a phone box (yes, the same person that the friendly, just-doing-my-job PC Pothole accused me of attacking!). The attacker was a blue-eyed, blond-haired man…which, as you might have worked out for yourselves, I am not. This experience, of course, didn't help the peace in my head and my absolute hatred of the police and any kind of authority.

Chapter Fourteen
and now, more physical pain

So let's move on a bit to a shortlist list of physical injuries. Apart from the many cuts, bruises and burns one gets as a headless chicken of a child – these were just a tad more serious.

At some point in the late seventies, I went out with my decorating partner and the boyfriend (who we shall call Frank) of my flat mate. We drove to Heathrow for a few drinks saying, 'If we get bored, we'll just go home'. Well I was bored almost immediately and soon joined by my partner. We told the now drunk, dancing Frank we were off and asked if he wanted a lift home. Too drunk and impolite, he just muttered some incoherent shit, so we left him to his own devices. After all, he was a grown man who could get home by himself - or so I thought.

I was awakened at 3 a.m. by Frank's girlfriend saying that he was lost, had no money and needed help. I dragged my ever-so-tired carcass out of the warmth of my bed and drove the few miles to find Frank and drive him home. As this simple task was far too complicated, I even took a spliff to cheer him up.

I found Frank wandering aimlessly, pulled up in the car, opened the door and said something like,

'Well thanks alot for dragging me out in the middle of the night, but never mind you're here now. Here's a nice fat spliff, let's go home.'

Instead of getting a polite, 'Well thanks mate, appreciate the help, the concern and especially thanks for the lovely spliff,' I just got a volley of drunken abuse, which I didn't take too well.

'Well fuck you,' I retorted and then added, 'One more word and you can stay here you ungrateful bastard'.

More words were exchanged.

'Right, you can just fuck right off,' I shouted as I got out of the car to open his door and throw the ungrateful Frank into the cold of the night. I was really angry, but even angrier that I still had drink inside me and really shouldn't have taken the risk of driving. After all, it's not beyond the wit of man to get a cab and get his girlfriend to pay when he returns.

He also got out of the car confronting me, and more words were exchanged. I was just about to punch him in the throat when I had a change of heart and just grabbed his throat while giving him the mother of all bollockings. Soon the bollocking was over and I said, 'Either get in the car of sod off'. As I turned - I think I must have slipped on the wet ground - I crashed to the floor and momentarily lost conscious as he repeatedly hit and kicked me in the face. I came to with Frank leaning over me with a face full of dripping madness, right hand raised with an axe about to strike, and screaming deranged obscenities.

I stood up, pushing him away as I did, and got back into the car. I checked my face in the rear view mirror as I wondered why I hurt so much and why I could taste blood.

Turns out I had a hole where my three front teeth used to be, a cut across the bridge of my nose, a swollen right eye, gash marks down my face and blood pouring from my wounds. I was furious. As I drove to the only hospital I knew, I tried to work out what had happened. My guess was that, as I fell, I hit my head on the ground so that's the scratch marks. The missing teeth I guessed must have been from the blunt side of the axe, and the other bruises were from being repeatedly kicked in the head. I hadn't felt a thing.

I drove to the A&E at Northwick Park Hospital where I was cleaned up and kept overnight. I asked them to contact my girlfriend, telling them I had been involved in a slight car accident; I certainly didn't want plod involved. My girlfriend duly arrived some hours later and burst into tears. I explained what really had happened. I moved out of the flat almost immediately and promised at some point in my life that I would get my revenge.

I stayed at my girlfriend's home for a week or so and my belongings were removed from my flat. I had heard through the grapevine that Frank was 'desperately sorry and regretted everything that he had done, but was drunk so he couldn't actually remember it.' We did eventually meet up where he fell to his knees sobbing, asking for forgiveness. I wasn't Jesus and I certainly wasn't in a forgiving mood then, and nor for many years to come.

Chapter Fifteen
First operation

The first operation was carried out at a dentist's training college at University College Hospital in London. I was strapped into a dentist's chair, covered from head to foot in green cloth, and given eight injections into my upper gum. That stung a little. Some ten minutes elapsed as the drugs took hold and then, with scalpel at the ready, the gum was sliced open. The student dental nurse hurried to cease the flow of claret. I thought that was bad - until I saw and heard the electric saw. The dentist approached with saw screaming and, like a scene from Marathon Man, my hands gripped the arms of the chair and my arsehole twitched like recent road kill. My hands gripped the chair tighter and tighter as sweat dripped from my furrowed brow. Screaming metal touched soft skin and then scythed into my upper gum until it cut into the bone.

The noise was unbearable and my heart banged like a shithouse door in a hurricane.

Although I felt no actual pain, I did feel and taste the blood slipping down my throat and the pressure of the metal saw against bone.

Soon the screaming noise ceased and there was silence as the nurse mopped up my blood. Then the torture continued with the dentist poking around and removing splinters of bone from inside my gum. I felt nauseous and faint while my heart continued its unhappy dance macabre.

My gum was sown up with sixteen stitches. My mouth ached, my head ached, and my heart was still beating so fast and so loudly that I thought I was about to have a heart attack. I got into my car and inspected the train wreck inside my mouth. I was horrified and felt like being sick. I had already reckoned on this so I had two fully loaded spliffs ready to smoke. I lit one up and relaxed back into the seat, allowing the rush to engulf me. I then drove slowly home and, unable to communicate, I just grunted like a pig. Some hours elapsed, the drugs wore off and then chronic pain ensued. I returned to work the next day feeling decidedly worse for wear.

Some months later, I returned to the dentist's training college to have my healed wound inspected and X rayed by Doctor Phibes and his evil henchwoman Cruella, only to be told,

'The operation was not successful and you will have to have another operation on the same (nicely healed) gum to rectify the problems of more broken bones that we somehow missed.'

Soon I was again sitting in the same chair, in the same room, in the same hospital with the same Doc Phibes and the same Nurse Cruella as they went through the exact same procedure. The green sheet covering me from head to toe, the same eight injections into the top gum, which still stung a little, the same scything scalpel, the same screaming saw, and the same masked psycho and his deranged student nurse hacking away at my face.

My hands slipped nicely back into the well-worn grip marks and my heart began drumming like a Ginger Baker drum solo and the sweat poured from my brow. This time I knew what was coming and it didn't help alleviate my trepidation. I shook like Elvis.

Once again I was stitched up and allowed home and again I sat in my car and smoked a large extra strong spliff. In fact, I think I had two. I again enjoyed the luxury of sucking baby food through a straw for the next week or two while my gums healed. Some months later, I was ordered to return and be checked again to see if this time they had managed to get it right - which they had failed to do the first time round. Much to my amazement and audible relief they said,

'That this time the operation was successful', and another appointment was made for some ill-fitting false teeth to be nailed into my mouth. At a much later date my nice new shiny grey teeth were fitted. It's not surprising then that my greatest fear is the dentist.

Not long after this injury I lacerated my hand on a glass door panel, which resulted in a drive to A&E where I had the shards of glass removed from the inside of my hand while sitting there watching. The sight was really quite unbearable, (the nurse was lovely) and the pain was almost unbearable. Although I still went back to work, the pain was terrible and it was terrible for months. I was eventually booked for surgery as an X-ray had found foreign objects still inside my hand. My right hand was operated on and a few large shards of glass were removed. I lost the use of some of the senses on the ledge of my hand as the cut had severed some nerves.

CHAPTER SIXTEEN
OH NO NOT ANOTHER INJURY

I had quit the decorating game, as I was bored senseless; bored with the long hours and bored by the sheer boredom of the entire boring job. I was offered the chance to work for someone else for a change, far away from the self-employed decorating game. I was offered a job as a specialist asbestos stripper, and the work was hard and tough but great fun. That soon changed as after only four months into the job, I got badly injured.

This came in the shape of a particularly nasty foot injury. The foreman and good friend Mark dropped, from approximately twenty feet, a very large and very heavy pebble dashed-coated asbestos sheet, which fell like a guillotine and smashed into my right foot, crushing and slicing it almost in two.

We're not sure how he managed this, but we were packing up for the day, transferring all the day's asbestos sheets from scaffolding to skip. Some sheets were 6' x 6' and others just 3' x 6', and each was passed down through cold hands from man to man with a shout of 'yeah got it' if the next person had it under their control.

I was on the ground level with two men on each elevation, and Mark was at the top. He went to pass a 3' x 6' panel to Fat Wallet and said that he thought he heard Fat Wallet say 'yeah got it'. Unfortunately, Fat Wallet hadn't, and Mark had just let go of an eighty kilogram asbestos sheet covered with pebble dash. It fell as described so eloquently earlier and landed on my right foot which only had trainers on - yes trainers, and not steel toe capped boots.

There was a brief millisecond as the foot sent the message to my brain to scream and while that was happening, I had thrown the eighty kilogram sheet of pebble-dashed-coated sheet of asbestos across the front garden in anger and then…

…and then I screamed like a sissy Mary as the immense pain hit me. I fell on to the ground as blood spurted out of my trainers. Malcolm rushed over and picked me up like he was picking up a baby and then gently threw me into the car while others ran around like headless chickens, really unsure of what to do.

'Malcolm, roll me a spliff,' I asked through gritted teeth, trying hard not to show the immense pain that coursed through my shaking body. In seconds it duly arrived. I took in lungful after lungful to shut out the pain as my mates gathered around trying to get a better look at my newly rearranged foot. The ambulance arrived with sirens blaring.

'Hold on lads, can I just finish this spliff off?' I asked the ambulance crew as I inhaled lungful after lungful of pain killer spliff - they did look a tad bemused at my odd request. Joint finished in record time, I was lifted gently into the ambulance as I waved a cheery 'Toodlepip chaps' to the amassed audience and soon I was being driven away at high speed while I sucked in lashings of oxygen. All I could do was grin.

Most people I guess would be screaming in pain, but I grinning inanely with the mixture of oxygen and dope as we drove to John Radcliffe Hospital. I asked the ambulance man while he cut away at my trainers if I had lost my foot. He told me after a few seconds inspection that I hadn't, but that it was a bloody mess. This was very reassuring. We duly arrived and I was pushed into the warmth and bright lights of A&E, where I was then seen by a host of Doctors and nurses and given all sorts of drugs. Not that I needed them; add morphine to the menu and I was off my face. I spent a week on my back in hospital, with my foot hung high and the wound left open to heal.

Malcolm and the lads arrived to visit and generally take the piss. Malcolm, God bless him, had baked me a spliff cake, which went down very well, especially when I gave the unsuspecting patients in my ward a slice and then happily watched them slowly reduced to giggling children and not knowing why. Malcolm had pointed at a small section of the cake and warned, 'This part has something very special in it'.

'Ok, I'll save that for the last day,' I replied smiling.

Well the last night had arrived and I was looking forward to a nice hot shower in a wheelchair, hoping and praying to God that my large-breasted nurse would come and hose me down. No chance; I was unceremoniously wheeled into the shower cubicle and the cold shower turned on as I fumbled with my hospital dressing gown, you know the ones where your arse sticks out the back. Soon back into bed and warmed, I decided to eat the final slice of the cake, wondering what on earth it could be, and knowing Malcolm, I thought it might well be Gorilla vomit or worse. I ate the cake and waited for something nice to happen. Well something nice did happen - I fell asleep. I awoke the next morning with the noise of a hundred voices echoing around my hazy head. I slowly opened my eyes to be greeted with about twenty student doctors/nurses inspecting my still open, very bloody sore wound. I soon realised that I was grinning from ear to ear and didn't really feel connected to my body. I covered my silly grinning face from the audience as it then occurred to me what Malcolm had put in that last slice of hash cake: mushrooms. Oh no not those kind of mushrooms you would normally get with egg, bacon, sausage, chips and beans and two of toast; oh no, these were the 'highly off your face naughty mushrooms' and they were 'exceptionally naughty.'

'You seem very happy Mr. Wheeler' the Doc commented.

'Oh yes,' I replied giggling inanely.

'In fact, you've been one of the happiest patients we've ever had Mr. Wheeler,' the Doc added.

'Yes I'm sure I have been,' I replied, thinking probably best I don't explain the hash cake and mushrooms. I was told that I could go home later after my aching foot was bandaged up.

After seven very uncomfortable and painful days, it was time to go. I said a cheerful goodbye to my 'still unknowing and what was in that cake?' friends on the ward as Lou and Malcolm arrived to take me home.

It was when I left in a wheelchair that I suddenly realized the seriousness of this injury. I couldn't bloody walk; I certainly wasn't going back to work anytime soon, and to make matters a tad more difficult, I lived in a flat on the second floor. I wasn't allowed to stand on my foot, which had to be raised above my head at all times. Trying to drop my daily mud monkeys was fun personified, but worse still I had no income, couldn't cook, couldn't walk, couldn't go out, couldn't do shopping, couldn't do diddly squat. In short, I was buggered but determined to get better and return to some sort of work. This was a serious injury and it took a very long time to heal enough to walk, and the pain was intense.

Some two years slowly elapsed and I was turning mental, not eating properly, no money, and bored shitless, sitting in my bloody room getting more and more hacked off and more and more angry. I had to do something before I exploded. I managed to get some cash in hand working as a no-questions-asked dodgy driver for some right dodgy geezers. The less said about that the better, but it brought some extra cash and got me out of my cave, but my foot still ached. In fact, I did anything I could as the benefit system was only paying me £29 per week, but my landlady was happy to get her rent. Guess who my landlady was - yes my mother, who tore any remaining emotions to ribbons. I couldn't even afford to eat, let alone anything else, but she still demanded I pay the rent. Then she'd brag about, 'I've got a new microwave fridge, etc.' I was furious.

I also revisited the notion of the army as a way out, not really thinking properly as I couldn't walk without limping. Nevertheless, I applied and soon found myself with a bunch of macho men running up a hill in Wales. I was hopeless, and when I say hopeless, I mean hopeless… but give me ten out of ten for effort. I lasted the first day and then had to listen to part-time, macho, weekend soldier boys bragging about exactly how 'hard they were'. It was like kindergarten for anally retentive morons. I wished I hadn't bothered to join, but having said that, it was fun. Perhaps it was the freedom and the memory of 'Hey I used to be good at this shit,' that spurred me on.

The next day was the similar to the first: run up that and run down that, climb that then climb off that, wade through that shit then wade out of that shit. Many were falling by the wayside, but for some odd reason I didn't. Well, not until we got back to what was described as camp, when we were systematically either told 'we stay or we go'. I failed, with the words 'good effort but too slow and that foot injury doesn't help' endorsement ringing in my ears. How did they know about the foot injury I wondered as I sat on the train station with a bunch of other failed recruits, being told by one guy that, 'There was no shame being kicked out after forty eight hours; most men who are army-trained don't last one hour with these guys.'

According to this bloke, whose face was made from teak, this was no ordinary outfit.

'I'll try another time 'I whispered under my breath, but that's yet another story.

Some months later, I went on a driver bodyguard course, which was anal.

So let's have a break from this detritus and let me tell you a story for no other reason except that's its funny.

Steve, Jon and I decided to go out for a drink, I drove my aging mini and we started off in the Production Village. We all drank Guinness and soon the pain of my foot and the depression I was experiencing dissipated. I was being careful not to drink too much. I knew my limits and if I kept control of myself, I knew with a spliff or two, I was safe to drive. We jumped into the mini and a couple of spliffs were rolled as we headed up to the Purple Pussycat in Finchley - the spliff was relaxing and I felt sober, unlike Steve and Jon. We duly arrived and set about drinking yet more. As soon as you could say 'leave it out lads' Jon and Steve were at each other's throats and soon punches and kicks were the order of the day. I just stood there like a moron trying to ignore the two baying bulls. Well, within a few minutes the bouncers had unceremoniously thrown out Jon and Steve while I was politely ushered outside.

I had parked my car close and with caution climbed into the passenger door (I'll explain why later) and moved over to the driver's side. I quickly put the skins together for a much needed spliff as Jon climbed in after, but there was no sign of Steve.

'Where's Steve? I asked

'Fuck him,' was the short sharp reply.

I finished rolling the spliff and Jon and I took very little time in demolishing it. My foot was really hurting so I decided shoe and sock off and hung the sock onto the rear view mirror as we drove off towards home.

When we neared Kilburn, I decided I needed to have another spliff so I pulled up and set about putting one together.

'There's a car reversing towards us' Jon said mid conversation.

I peered through the steamy windows to see the reversing lights and then, the Police lights. 'Oh fuck' I whispered and quickly took the keys out of the ignition, tossed them on to the back seat and threw the beginnings on my half made spliff onto the floor.

A male plod got out of the driver's side and a female plod got out of the passenger side and promptly walked over to my door. I slid open the window and a conversation ensued which went something like,

'Hello Officer, what can I do for you?'

'What are you doing here?' he asked completely ignoring my polite question.

'I'm just sitting here talking to my friend,' I replied,

'Why are you sitting here?' he asked, this time less polite.

'Because we've been at a party down the road and we wanted a chat,' I replied.

'Right, get out of the car'.

'Don't open the door, it will fall off,' I pleaded.

He went to open the door. Again I pleaded, 'Don't open the door, it will fall off'.

I said to Jon, 'Get out I want to talk to this fucking idiot.' Jon stumbled out, soon followed by a raging me, grabbing my shoe as I crawled out.

Both the plod officers looked a tad bemused at what I was doing and another conversation began.

'Why didn't you get out of your side?' the idiot plod asked, yet again.

'Because the fucking door will fall off'.

'Have you been drinking'?

'Yes'.

'Were you driving the car'?

'No, I just explained, I was at a party'.

'Right, you're nicked,' he shouted. I lost it and went for him while Jon struggled to keep me back as I ranted. The back up plod soon arrived.

I was then unceremoniously dragged across the road and thrown into the back of the foul-smelling, puke-filled meat wagon. This was followed rapidly by a few officers, who just laid into me, but as I was still pissed and didn't feel a thing. I was then driven at some pace to Kilburn Police Station, where I began again, where I left off, steaming with rage and anger at the thorough hiding I had just received from the plods.

The next morning arrived and I found myself half naked on

the cell floor, aching all over. I was soon sitting in front of the desk sergeant.

'So you want to make an official complaint do you? I suggest you are one lucky sod, so I will say that you should fuck off home now and count yourself-very lucky.'

My head swam as I tried to recall the night before and couldn't.

'Where's my car?'

'The keys are at Willesden Police Station, but don't think about picking them up as you won't be allowed to drive as you are still drunk and over the limit'.

I walked to Willesden Police Station; it was about 7 a.m.

'I've come to pick up the keys to my car,' I politely informed the plod at Willesden Police Station.

'No you can't have them, but just in case you are fit to drive, we will breathalyse you. You failed, oh and by the way, your gay friend got arrested last night as well, so now, fuck off.'

I walked out of the police station without my car keys and found a mini cab driver. Soon I was home where I went straight to bed, only to be rudely awoken by a grinning Steve banging on my front door.

'What happened to you?' he asked. I retold the story as far as I could remember.

'So what happened to you and where's Jon?'

'Someone phoned the plod as I was lying in the gutter, and they duly arrived and arrested me,' Steve replied.

'What for, lying in the gutter or for being fucking annoying'? I asked

'Both,' Steve replied smiling.

'So where's Jon?'Steve asked.

The phone rang. It was Jon.

'What happened to you? And what happened to Steve?' went the discussion. 'Tell you what, let's meet in an hour down the pub'.

One hour passed and all three of us, weary and tired, sat and discussed the night before. I told my story and then Jon told us his and this is how it went...

After seeing me being dragged, kicking and screaming, into the meat wagon, Jon decided stupidly to follow me, as my foot was still in bad shape. I guess he must have felt a brotherly, protective, drunk spirit towards me. He found the keys to my mini on the back seat and hastily drove off behind the blue flashing lights of the meat wagon. He got to Harlesden town centre, where he was stopped by a different set of plod. The plod went to open the driver's door. Jon pleaded like I did, Don't open driver's door'.

Sadly the plod wasn't listening and he opened the driver's door, which fell off in his hands - yes the entire door, only now held on by one very worn out strip of leather.

Jon was arrested for drunk driving, spent the night in the cells at Willesden Police Station and was subsequently charged with drunk driving; he then got a cab home, slightly pissed off.

'So Steve, what happened to you then?' Jon asked.

'I was arrested for being drunk and lying face down in the gutter and for possession of a small bit of spliff and was taken to West Hampstead Police Station'.

'Did they charge you for the spliff and being drunk and disorderly?' Jon enquired.

'No, they let me off for being annoying,' Steve replied grinning.

'Cunt' Jon replied.

'Annoying cunt,' I butted in.

'So where's your car Kim?' Jon and Steve asked.

'I don't know, I'll ask the last person who saw it. Where is my car Jon?'

'Harlesden, with the door hanging off, your sock hanging from rear view mirror and Vera Lyn's (skins) everywhere'.

'And where are the keys?' Steve asked.

'Willesden Police Station. I asked for them back but they said I was still pissed and told me in no uncertain terms to, fuck off'.

We sat laughing at the absurdity of all this, but then I had to get my car back. I rang a friend and asked for a lift, but I wasn't going to go back to the Police Station. So we drove to Midnight Motors and with a small deposit of a few quid got every conceivable mini car key known to man and drove off to find my old mini. There in all her glory was my mini, with door still hanging off, parked four feet from the curb in the middle of a Pelican crossing in the middle of Harlesden High Street.

'How the, what the fuck!!' I exclaimed as I opened the passenger door and climbed in with the assortment of mini keys. There, as Jon had said, was my sock still hanging off the rear view mirror, Vera Lyn's everywhere and, much to my surprise was a quarter of an ounce of the spliff I had last night still unwrapped sitting on the driver's seat.

'Result,' I shouted while people at the bus stop looked on, bemused as I managed to shut the driver's door, start the engine and roar off home, giggling like a child.

So to recap, three men went out for a quiet drink, three men got drunk and all three got arrested at three different times in three different locations and sent to three different police stations.

Steve got off for being fucking annoying. Jon got done for drunk driving and subsequently got two years ban. I walked away Scott free for being a loud, aggressive, full-of-fight fucking idiot Got my car back in one piece, my spliff not stolen and returned safely to rightful grinning owner (or for that matter, found by plod but with Jon luckily not charged with possession as well as drunk driving), my sock still attached to the rear view mirror and my mind thinking, what the fuck just happened.

We sat in the pub, re-telling the story to anyone who would listen and got hammered, yet again.

Jon and I went to court. We managed to get his sentence reduced to twelve months.

Some years later I got a part payment from insurers for my foot injury and with this money, I trained for a new job, HGV Class one - yes just what you do with a smashed, crushed, cut and buggered foot!

Chapter Seventeen
Oh you have got to be joking

Between trying to find a job I just did some odds and sods for people (some legal, mostly they were not). I was still useful with my hands and one day I was asked to help an old couple with their lawn. I was happily mowing away when I heard a dull crack in the base of my spine, feeling pain that was unbelievable. I managed to get home and tried not to worry about this scything pain. I will get back to this a bit later, but first I had an appointment with a new kind of instructor.

Soon I was on my mountain bike cycling the eight miles to Southall to have my first lesson in HGV Class One, driving heavy duty trucks. The Indian instructor met me, asking that I put my bike on the trailer and climb in. 'Passenger side' I whispered to myself, unsure of what he meant. I was soon put straight by, 'I know how to drive the bloody truck,' said the instructor in his broken English.

So every day for six days I had two hours of training, which was relatively easy and slightly easier than running up and down hills. On the seventh day I took the driving test. I reversed perfectly, I drove forwards perfectly, I braked perfectly and I got all the questions right as I had swotted like teacher's pet every waking hour.

'Congratulations Mr. Wheeler you have passed,' the test instructor climbed out of the cab and my instructor climbed in.

'Well done mate,' he said beaming from one ear to the next.

'Now all you have to do is get a job.'

Driving was probably not the best thing for an injured foot and I wasn't allowed to work off ladders. I had failed army selection with style, and no way was I going back into the building game. Using previous skills was now a no-go area. 'I'll take the pain,' I thought. I really just wanted to work and get my life back to as normal as possible. I went back to the doctor time and time again and every time he would just dismiss this agony as 'just back ache.'

Soon I was driving forty ton trucks with three axles and eighteen gears - the truck I trained on had just six gears. Suddenly life was great again. Although the hours were long and tiring and my foot/back ached and the pay was crap, I was, at least, on the road. I had plans for my future - to keep up this driving for a couple of years, get loads of experience, and soon do inter-continental driving.

My back pain worsened, sleep was almost impossible and work became far too painful, so again I found myself sitting in front of my computer fixated Doc, who then ordered me to cease working immediately. I was heartbroken.

I then spent the next two years trying to convince doctor after bloody doctor, expert after bloody expert, that my back was indeed injured. Nobody seemed, or indeed wanted to believe me. This resulted in my being sent from pillar to post where I was required to throw all types of shapes just for the amusement of these uninterested and uncaring doctors. Do this, do that, bend this, bend that, put your left foot here, put your right foot there, lift your leg, now lift the other leg up, try and touch your toes. You know an X-ray would have helped or even an MRI scan. I wondered why I wasn't afforded this small luxury because it would have found the problem, wouldn't it? Suddenly I was back to square one with no income, in great pain, sitting bored shitless in my grotty, dingy, cold flat as the short highs in my life slid slowly down the drain.

I was eventually sent to St. Vincent's hospital where I was asked to attend physio classes. As I walked in I noticed that everyone was well over one hundred years of age and the physio instructor was the most patronising woman I had ever had the misfortune to meet. We were soon at each other's throats as raising my legs in the air along with the Derby and Joan club simply wasn't what I required.

Eventually I was told that I should attend the same hospital to have something called a Mylogram, also known as a Radiculagram. A syringe full of an opaque liquid was inserted (with much difficulty and pain) into my lower spine by an alcohol-stinking, inebriated doc. I would then be placed on a swiveling table while my spine was X-rayed. I went through all the tests and was told to return to the ward.

Within two hours I started to feel sick, and within four, I was carted off in great haste to a darkened room where I vomited for the next twelve hours. My body went into spasms as I puked the entire contents of my guts out, along with yellow bile. My body would lift from the bed in a sort of exorcist-like spasm.

I was injected here, there and everywhere as doctors ran around like headless chickens. This sideshow continued for hours, my retching and sickness worsened, and every time I tried to close my eyes to sleep I got treated to the most evil, frightening hallucinations. My entire body was screaming in agony. It felt like I was on fire and the Doctors continued to pump more and more drugs into me. They then tried to put an injection into a vein in my arm. It missed, so now I had a swelling the size of a tennis ball. I couldn't rest. I couldn't sleep, I couldn't close my eyes. I couldn't even drink water as I would just throw it all up. For good measure, I was left in total darkness.

A day passed, then two, then three, by which time the hallucinations had got a whole lot worse. I didn't have to close my eyes as they were in the shadows of my darkened cell.

I was frightened because I just didn't know what was going on. As I lay there, I thought through my pains, about the life that I had been given and how I had ended up in the position I was in. I decided to pray to the invisible God. I asked, no I begged him to 'let me die.' I really had had enough and just couldn't take anymore suffering.

'Please God,' I pleaded, 'take me away from this pain and suffering; please God, just let me die.'

For some odd reason during that night I had asked a nurse to open the curtains and, while I was just goofing out of the window at the trees bending with the breeze, an oval light suddenly appeared above the tree nearest my window.

'Bloody hallucinations,' I said to myself. I blinked a few times to rid myself of this vision but it didn't go away. The oval light was four to five feet wide and I guess about three foot high. I was mesmerized by it, or was I cracking up? Suddenly out of the gloom a gentle voice of a man said,

'You're going to be all right.'

'Who is that?' I whispered into the darkness.

'I am God, your father.'

I then just fell to pieces and wept uncontrollably, blabbing away with one of those long sticky snots hanging, swaying to and fro out of my nose. After some lengthy discussions with this man who called himself God, the light above the tree disappeared and the voice of God fell silent, and again I was plunged into darkness, numb and slightly bemused by what had just occurred.

I then realized that I wasn't alone. There was man standing next to me dressed from head to toe in black and talking in what I guessed was Latin. Was he giving me the last rites? Or ordering me a takeaway Pizza? And why was there a priest in my room?

'Was I was dying!' I whispered to myself.

I thought about this troubled situation, I thought about past battles, I thought about the visit from God and the positive words of encouragement. Though I was still shaken and shaking with the content of the conversation I just had with God, I just couldn't get my head around God calling me his son.

As I lay there alone in the darkness and gloom, I thought about my survival and my spirits lifted. I really didn't want to die. I wanted to live, I wanted to fight, and I wanted to get better and I wanted to get out of this bloody hospital.

On this very same day I was not allowed any visitors. I believed that even the doctors had given up on me. Luckily for me, God had not.

Within a few hours I began to feel less scared as I sipped at some cold water. Within forty eight hours I had eaten my first slice of cold, dry toast. I began to feel better, the hallucinations dissipated. On the sixth day, I slept well, but soon my much needed slumbers were rudely interrupted by the physiotherapist and a nurse, who threw back the curtains, blinding me with light while the physiotherapist removed all of my bed sheets, leaving me naked, while demanding,

'Which leg is injured'?

They soon left after I gave them both a mouthful. I noticed that she had left an assortment of walking aids and I also noticed my body was not the one I came into hospital with. I was horrified as I glanced at my normally fit, muscular, athletic body; what I was looking at was just skin and bones.

Some hours later 'she bitch the physio' returned, but this time a tad less enthusiastic and a tad more polite, leaving me with just a Zimmer frame. A few hours elapsed and, for the first time in six days, I got out of bed and hobbled about clutching the Zimmer frame. I could hardly walk. I found the scales and weighed myself, and to my disbelief weighed nine stone three.

The nightmares and hallucinations disappeared in time, but most importantly, I was alive, just barely.

I felt I had God on my side and a friend in Karen, my new landlady (Yes, I had to move out of my hovel to get enough money to live, while my mother still took her rent). I still felt and looked like death, but I was eventually allowed home. Karen picked me up and I saw her quietly shed a tear as I struggled to walk the few yards to the awaiting car and freedom. I don't know how I would have coped if I had still lived alone at home. She was an angel and I was a wreck.

In a few months the pain eased, my eyesight and hearing reverted to the norm rather than the twenty-twenty vision and the hearing of a bat. All my senses had been heightened for months. I thought I had turned into Spiderman.

Confess…

I must confess
That my world was a mess
And nobody knew who I was
I am friendless and alone
And live on my own
My world is painful and empty
I survive this life
With no lovers or a wife
And no children to call me daddy
I struggle each day
To fight the impossible way
To stop myself-going crazy
I have one last chance
To learn the steps to life's dance
Or perhaps, curl up and be forgotten
I called out to the skies
'Please God help me survive'
And a voice came out of heaven
'Son, I will hold tight your hand
And be your best friend,
Today, tomorrow and ever
I will help you survive
Keep all of your dreams alive
Son, live all your new plans
Remember who I am
And I will love you forever'.

I still had to find a cure and the reason for my back pain, and after six more months of pleading, begging, groveling at the feet of my uninterested GP, I was finally invited to have an MRI scan at Northwick Park Hospital.

This was just a tad scary, being pushed backwoods into the belly of this massive machine whilst it banged like a jack hammer. But they found the problem and I was deranged with happiness, and it did make me think;

'Why didn't they do that right after my injury rather than making me wait in agony for over three years?'

Within just nine months of almost dying at St. Vincents Hospital I was booked into Stanmore Hospital. I didn't think my body could cope with yet more pain, but I didn't have any choice. I just held my breath and got on with it.

I was wheeled into the operating theatre and was given a horse tranquilizer. 'Count back from one hundred, Kim,' the nurse said calmly.

'99, 98 ...' I was out.

I awoke some time later in excruciating agony, curled up like a foetus with this contraption attached to my arm. I blindly fumbled with this apparatus and then I found a plunger.

'Oh I know what this is,' I said smiling. 'Morphine, Planet Zanusi, here I come.'

Suddenly I was buzzing and the pain disappeared for a few hours. Again and again I pushed the plunger in for more lovely morphine then just lay back and grinned.

A man's voice came out of the gloom asking,

'You alright mate'?

I opened my bleary eyes and looked around trying to locate where and who the sound was coming from.

'You alright mate?' the voice repeated. I again looked around and finally located the source. It was a grinning patient across the ward, who had broken his spine weight lifting.

I was later told that I had had four metal bolts inserted into my back and wire to hold my lower spine together, and that I would be staying in hospital for a further thirteen days.

'Oh, no I won't. I want out.'

Six days later and feeling good enough to venture to the toilet and also to talk to the guy who woke me from my slumbers, I was informed by the nurse that if I could climb some stairs with no problems, I could go home the very next day. I reminded myself of Douglas Bader's heroics and I climbed those stairs with ease. The very next day, as promised, I was saying goodbye to all my new friends and nurses, hoping that I would never see or have to hear or smell their arse trumpets again.

Some weeks had passed when I was informed that I wasn't allowed to do anything for at least TWO YEARS. That went down well. I was also told that there was a strong possibility that I might need walking sticks and, worse still, a wheelchair. I was also warned about chronic pain, and the possibility that all this might last for the rest of my life. Oh Joy!!!

Two years of madness, pain, boredom and frustrations slowly elapsed and I was ordered to see the back surgeon. He looked at my X-rays and calmly said,

'Your back operation was not a success. You have a failed back and there is nothing more that we can do. Goodbye'.

My head swam in treacle as I tried to take in what the Doc just said. I punched myself in the face to make sure I wasn't having another nightmare, much to the amusement of the other passengers on the train. My dingy world fell to bits, yet again.

Again I found myself sitting in front of my computer fixated Doc.

'Doc, I need some help,' I pleaded.

Chapter Eighteen
On the road to nowhere

I was then sent from pillar to post. I was sent to 'drug addicts r us' where I sat waiting in a corridor full of smack heads and low life losers. God, I felt depressed. I was invited into a private room to talk to some bloke whose name escapes me and, after a few minutes, we both realised that I was in the wrong place, talking to the wrong person about all the wrong things. This was a centre for complete anally retentive fuckwits and even I, wasn't that fucked up.

After that wasted session, I soon found myself sitting in front of my computer-fixated Doc and I wasn't bloody happy. All this did was to pile more misery on to my already pissed-off, raging and very angry mind.

I was eventually sent to another so-called therapist. This one worked in psychiatry. Soon I was sitting in another morbid-looking waiting room in the bowels of Northwick Park Hospital surrounded by three chain-smoking, wall-eyed, spotty, applied-make-up-with-chainsaw, cackling slappers.

'Got a fag mate'? 'Got a fag mate? We only want a fag, mate'.

I turned to confront these hag-ridden harridan witches and unleashed one of my better verbal assaults, which resulted in security arriving and carting these three insanely mad bitches back to looneyland where hopefully they were shot. I really wasn't in a very good mood.

I reminded myself of what I was going to say to the

psychiatrist when this man appeared apparently out of nowhere. With keys jangling from his belt, he invited me to follow him.

He unlocked two doors into the corridor from hell, then through another locked door, to the most dismal wrist-slitting room from Hades that I ever had the misfortune to sit in. He sat down, told me to sit down, and then stared at me without saying a single word. My head raced; in my mind I jumped up and ran to his desk screaming,

'I seem to have a problem with anger!' and knocked the eye-fighting psychiatrist clean out.

When I came back to reality, this eye-fighting beginner was still staring at me. What he hadn't realised was that when it came to eye-fighting, I was a fucking Jedi master and could burn my name into steel from a thousand yards. This man was just putty in my hands, poor sap! My fists clenched, my head spun and I felt I was about to erupt. I then politely screamed,

'What the fuck are you staring at?'

'I need you to talk, open up, and to say what's on your mind.'

'What's on my mind? What do you think is on my fucked-up loony tooney wavy gravy mind?'

'I don't know,' he replied sarcastically and arrogantly.

'Then why don't you read my case notes and then we can stop having all this sex and get on with the real issues?' I replied.

I was trying so hard to keep calm and not lose the plot but sadly it was too late; I lost it big time. I suddenly stood up and he flinched as if I was about to attack him. Then I tried to march out of this dismal depressing cell, not realising that I was locked in. I turned to face him.

'Get me the fuck out of here!' I quietly demanded.

Stinking Pit…

I was sitting in a stinking pit
Full of others peoples' shit
I had no voice, I did not fit
I held my nose and got used to it
Then one day the time had come
To change my life, I start to run
Far away from the darkened sun
I found myself, then had some fun
So farewell to the nauseous smell
The stench of failure is a lonely hell
I have a plan as you can tell
I'm standing tall, where I first fell.

Soon I was out into the bright sunshine and the warmth and freedom of a rare sunny afternoon. It's not surprising why so many people who go through this debacle end up barking mad. So guess what happened next? Correct, I sat twitching in front of my Doc again as he still continued to stare at his computer. This time I had magma erupting from my ears, blood dripping from my nose and saliva dripping from the corner of my twitching mouth. I was seriously losing it.

Some months later I was invited back to Northwick Park Hospital, but this time I was to attend a pain clinic. I readied myself for another trip to hell but was surprised when I was sent to a nice, bright waiting room where the charming nurse Angie, came out and spoke to me in a lovely, friendly, polite manner. She even called me Kim.

'The Doc will see you now, Kim,' she said charmingly.

I walked in to see the Doc, who introduced herself to me as Doctor Laurie Allen. I spoke and she listened intently. I told her of my last few attempts at getting some help and that my Doc seemed more interested in his computer than he was in talking to me. I was asked to return some weeks later for some hypnotherapy. I actually left her feeling elated and couldn't wait to return.

Some weeks later, I returned and lay on a bed as this bloke began chanting some spurious old nonsense and I promptly fell asleep. No, this isn't working either.

Soon I was sent to another part of Northwick Park Hospital to see a clinical psychologist, whatever that is. Again I sat in another dreary corridor, and again thinking about what to say. Soon my name was called and I dragged my useless carcass to its feet to meet this voice.

'Hello Kim, my name is Doctor Elaine McWilliams and I'm your Clinical Psychologist.'

She was five foot nothing, blond, pretty and far removed from the wall-eyed harridans and the trainee eye-fighting Muppet that I had encountered before.

We sat in a grey box room where I was introduced to a student who was doing her thesis on pain. I was asked some personal questions and soon I was flooding the room with years of painful memories. All too soon my hour was up.

'Same time next week, Kim,' she said whilst smiling that reassuring, caring smile.

I instantly trusted her.

Chapter Nineteen
The pain clinic

We first talked about the catalogue of physical injuries and then briefly discussed the physical abuses by my adopted Mother. I told Dr. McWilliams everything I could remember. This, sadly, had a detrimental effect on me. Reliving all these bad memories made me feel worse, but, as you'll read often in this book, I had to go backwards to go forwards, and I wasn't going to give up. I had found a good person who genuinely seemed interested in helping me understand my life story and wild horses could not drag me away.

She told me that she thought I was hiding something from my past, which was true. She asked me to open up and not be frightened; after all she was there to help. I really didn't want to discuss my deepest emotions with a relative stranger but I knew that if I wanted help then I had to let her know everything.

We discussed my first five years, my desertion by my birth Mother and the children's home. We talked and talked with a million questions from both sides, which brought the entire gambit of my emotions to the discussions. I was left angry, sad, hacked off, emotionally exhausted and bitter with realizations of exactly how shit my life had been and how I really needed to change everything.

We journeyed into my past and talked about my birth parents. My Mother became pregnant; my birth Father wanted nothing to do with any of it so she was left to deal with the responsibility alone. We found out at a much later date that she had been very young, homeless, potless, unwell and in no fit state to bring me up. I came out of her womb a tad too dark and society looked down on her for mating unmarried with a non-white man, which was just not acceptable to society.

Her life must have been hell. I felt for her, so didn't blame her for what she did. I just missed having her around. My birth Father, I just didn't care about.

We talked about the chances of tracing my birth parents but I knew from an early age that I never really wanted to do this. I suppose because I felt so rejected and unloved that there seemed no reason to find them, plus they might well have rejected me again.

Much later on, I did put myself on a register to find out if anyone had been looking for me. The response was negative, which hurt a little. I was sort of hoping that in my fifty plus years on Planet Earth just one person wondered where I was and how I was doing. There was nobody. I did, however, find out that I had a half sister who had also been abandoned. Sadly, my birth Mother was not even aware if I was alive or dead, and probably never will.

We also spoke about my adopted parents, what they did, when they did it, my brothers and sister, schooling, memories, achievements, holidays, where I stood in the pack as the youngest, my feelings towards them and their feelings towards me, and how I felt that all I had done was bring pain into their perfect lives. I told Elaine that I was only with this family for six years before I was sent to boarding school. My brothers and sister were leaving their schools and either going to college or university when I first went to mine, so after that I didn't get to see them much. During holidays they would be away and I would be sent to adventure holiday camps. When I did leave school at age fifteen, they had all moved away and the family home was empty. I only got the best of them for a comparatively short time, certainly not long enough to get to know them. We did, however, occasionally meet up at Christmas, but soon I didn't even bother going to that.

Once a week I would prepare myself mentally for my next appointment, sometimes excited with the prospect of seeing Elaine and sometimes dreading it. Before I even got to sit in front of Elaine, I would often be stressed to breaking point with the impossible task of finding a parking space. Although I had my blue badge, there were only about ten spaces in car parks big enough for a thousand cars. More times than not, some grubby little shit with a car full of insidious ugly children would be parked in the only free disabled bays.

More often than not, I just couldn't find any space and so I had to pay. Not only did I have to prepare myself for the mental battle of my life, I had to make sure I had the correct change and leave in plenty of time. No, not the hardest task in the world I readily admit, but when you're in a state of razor blade walking, it was really important to have these minor irritants sorted the night before . I didn't want to spoil a good hour with tales of ineptitude and rage.

Elaine would know as soon as I walked into her office if it was going to be a good session or not. I would often walk in steaming with rage, quite ready to jump out the window. Sometimes my anger just got too much and I would leave in seconds, even more angry then when I had arrived. Poor Elaine would have the look of someone who had just walked through a one hundred year storm. This made me feel like a complete shit. She was, after all, trying to help me, so the next time I would try that bit harder. Not all the appointments were mental and often we would both have a good laugh at the absurdity of life and its irritants, but this was as rare as rocking horse shit.

We spoke at length about pain management, how pain worked, gates, circles of anger, stress, and depression resulting in anger. Sometimes I would understand, sometimes I just couldn't. Sometimes I wanted to shout at my weaknesses, insecurities and my hatred of having to hear all about my issues and problems, which I still felt were handed down to me, but mostly I just wanted to cry.

I explained to Elaine how I did try to get along with my adoptive parents but never seemed able to, and still felt that I was not up to the same standards as their own children who really excelled at University. In my parents' eyes I just didn't excel at anything, except being a little shit.

There were still things my Mother did to reinforce this fear. I was never allowed a front door key, I had to be home at a certain time or be locked out. If I did stay out late, I would have to sneak into the garage and sleep in the car, which was ice-cold during winter. She knew I was doing this but showed little or no interest or motherly care. This was clear as daylight when I went out one night with friends and ended up at a party. My drink was spiked and I fell unconscious. I was then unceremoniously dumped outside my parents' house as my friends were too scared to knock on the door. I was found blue and shivering the next morning by the neighbors. I was carried into the house, where I stayed in the same unconscious state for two more days. My Mother only rang the doctor when I finally woke up. After I was given a check over, the Doctor berated my Mother as I could have died. I honestly think that she just couldn't have cared less, and that's how our relationship continued.

Chapter Twenty
Death

One day I got a message from my Mother that my Father had been taken ill. This was about a week or perhaps longer after the rest of my family had been informed. I was told that he was in hospital but was fine and sitting up chatting to the nurses. I asked if I could visit and a time was arranged. I walked into the ward only to see my Mother sitting next to a grey, shaking skeleton. I almost fainted on the spot as my mind raced to understand the difference between her assurances that 'he was all right, sitting up and cheerily chatting with the nurses' and the apparition lying before me. This was certainly not cheery or chatting, but was very close to death. I stumbled towards his bed and put my hand on his almost cold hand. I looked searchingly into my Mother's ice-cold eyes, searching for a flicker of emotion, guilt or betrayal at the lie she had told me.

'Does he know I'm here?' I asked.

'Yes,' she replied unemotionally.

I looked at him. His eyes were shaking from side to side, he was gaunt and skinny, and did not resemble the memory I had of my Father as an overweight man. This man had obviously been ill for ages.

Why hadn't they told me? My anger levels rose. I stood up, looked at my Mother with tears in my eyes, walked out of the ward and just slumped in a heap in the busy corridor. I honestly thought I was going to pass out.

After a few minutes, and some dirty looks from the staff, I got up, reminded the nurses 'that was my Father dying in there.' I walked over to the bed and said to my still unemotional and silent Mother, 'I have to go, let me know when I can see him again.'

I squeezed his hand and left.

That night I went to the pub to get absolutely bladdered. On returning home, I found a crumpled bit of paper that had been stuffed through the front door and lay sadly alone on the hall floor. The message said, 'Your Father passed away at nine.'

I went upstairs and rolled spliff after spliff until I was numb. I continued to wonder why I hadn't been told of my Father's illness before and in more honest detail. My Father had paid for everything for me: food, clothing, schooling, holidays, etc. I felt ashamed that I never got the chance to say 'thank you' for his kindness and generosity. As for my Mother, I only had more resentment, almost hatred, and yet more anger.

My Father had had a massive stroke and nobody could be bothered to tell me. Again, the feeling of not being wanted and not a part of this family reared its plug ugly face.

Some years later, I was told that my Mother was ill in hospital with cancer. Again, I arranged a visit and met up with my sister who had flown down from Scotland. I walked in to the single room where my Mother was lying propped up by pillows. I sat next to my Mother and waffled on about the garden and any old bollocks because asking…

'Well how are you?' would be met with the derision it deserved.

I felt very uncomfortable, as if I wasn't really wanted there. I was asked to go and get her a newspaper, which seemed a very strange request. Obedient to the last, I obeyed, thinking it was just a ruse to get me away. I came back within five minutes but I had already made the decision to go. I looked into my Mother's eyes searching for a glimpse of emotion or love, but I just got the same unemotional look back.

I smiled and said 'that I would try and see her later' rather than utter something deep and meaningless. We both understood this sentiment as it was easier for us to deal with this departure in the old fashioned way of 'don't show any emotions or pain'. What I really wanted was to hug her and tell her that 'I loved her,' but I couldn't because I didn't love her and probably never had. I had tried harder than anyone else to receive just a modicum of love back. What I wanted her to do, she wouldn't or couldn't, so it was a stalemate.

My sister accompanied me downstairs where we sat in the canteen. Probably for the first time in my life, I expressed my honest views about our Mother and what she had done to me, emotionally and physically. I knew this was not easy for my sister to hear. She said that Mother had 'admitted to her that there had been mistakes in my upbringing'. Shame that she forgot to explain that one to me! It might just have helped heal the many scars that I carried.

My Mother died some hours later and all I felt was relief, perhaps because she had gone to sleep in peace or that she could no longer hurt me. It may sound terrible but that's what I felt, just relief. I did't mourn her death like I mourned my Father's, nor did I cry, but funnily enough, whilst deep in thought and in forgiving mode, I did manage to say a silent, 'thank you.'

I honestly believed that she thought that what she had done was correct and was best for me and in some odd way she had been right. I didn't like her strictness, hated the beatings, the coldness and her empty, unemotional heart. It might have been better and easier for me and my emotions if it was accompanied with hugs and heaps of love. It hadn't been like that, and I guess that is just fucking tough.

I did find out later that even my other brother, the second eldest, apparently also failed to make certain grades set by our Mother's criticizing his music, his hair, his drug taking.

I have often felt guilty for my weakness and inability to be good enough. Sometimes I would ask myself, 'was it better to be humiliated by this Mother or to have no Mother at all and would the pain of loneliness be better than total annihilation?' I guess the answer is that I preferred to take the pain - but only just! In truth I don't miss her, which in itself, is sad.

Some three years had elapsed when I was informed that I could no longer see Elaine because some supervisor had decided that our time was up. Elaine and I had covered a lot of ground. I was now seeing her on a monthly basis. We had covered the past and the present. We covered nearly everything, every wrong and every right, all manner of pains and my inabilities to see or indeed face the truth. I learned from her and I guess she learned from me. We didn't deal with me facing the future. I guess that was really up to me. I felt that, because of all her help in covering the past, I would still need her guiding hand, but in reality it was time for me to fly. She showed me an old saying which said:

'Go to the edge,' the man said,
'No,' I replied,
'Go to the edge,' the man said again,
'No, I am too scared.'
'Go to the edge,' the man finally said.
So I went to the edge and he pushed me –
And I flew.

Soon I was hugging Elaine a very tearful goodbye. I was now on my own, and had yet another installment of life's war to face, endure and ultimately conquer. I felt weak but strong, lost but found, and a whole lot happier. What would I have done without her help? I just don't know…probably wearing a straight-jacket and giving those three achingly-ugly, chain-smoking, cackling harridans my telephone number.

Then just to test me further, life gave me another kick in my head: my brother Jonathan got Cancer. Four years later we buried him. I was in shock, numb, very sad and angry, all at once. Yet again, the bitch called life came to give me another sound hiding. Then just to add a bit more grief to my already embittered life, my second dog Purdy became ill and as with Pod, I had to put to him sleep.

I was edging myself to the top of my darkened pit. Now I could see the light, in fact almost touch it, but there was still a very long way to go. I wasn't ever going to give up. I felt invincible, and I would need to be. I reminded myself of how far I had come and a saying that I had read,

'What lies behind us and what lies before us are nothing compared to what lies within us'.

Shit Creek…

I wake up sometime a.m.
Then paddle down shit creek
Shit, it's only Monday
The beginning of the week
I fall out of bed and rub my head
Then scratch at my three piece suite
Pick the Randolph Scotts from my boat race
And remove the black bit from my feet
Put on my suit of armour
That protects me through this day
Remind myself of who I am
Prepared, I'm on my way
But my road is made of quicksand
And my boots are full of lead
Emptiness fills my stomach
And there's weird shit in my head
I've wasted endless chances
That came knocking at my door
I'm just too fucking lazy
To get my useless carcass off the floor
My shadow tells me to get a grip
Then my mind says, oh what's the point
Go home and put your feet up
And smoke another joint.

Chapter Twenty One
Self-healing

Now we have to discuss the self-healing process along with the many wars I had to face before I could become a free, content and a happy man. I had to climb out of my pit and face everything that I had not faced before. I didn't know how long this journey would take or indeed how painful it was going to be. Perhaps if I had known the height of the mountains I had to climb, I would have bottled out. But it was a journey I just had to make. It was my life at stake here and nobody could repair the years of damage except me.

Stage One...Government Benefits

(Remember this occurred some years ago, whether the benefit system has improved or not I'm not sure. I somehow doubt it but you will soon find out if you are in need of help) Getting the entitled benefits took an unbelievable THREE years and was a war of attrition in itself - with form filling, telephone calls to unhelpful nobodies at the DHS who steadfastly refused to listen, constant rejection and more form filling and rudeness. It was almost impossible, and when you are told that you are entitled to help and find yourself treated in such an abysmal way, it's no wonder people get angry and stressed.

In the end, I gave up with them, which I believe they wanted to happen on purpose, and then sought help and guidance at a local disability centre, and they were brilliant. They sat me down and reassured me of my entitlements and even helped with the form filling. They showed me there is a correct way to do it and an incorrect way not to do it, and if you get the form filling wrong, you will not get the help you deserve.

Eventually I was ordered up to London with a member of this disability centre to sit in front of a board of three people: I believe a Doctor, a Solicitor and a dead pelican. I walked into the room and there they were perched up high in large seats. I was told to sit in a little chair below them - talk about feeling inferior! I sat like a good boy and was given the chance to explain my injuries with prompting from the lady from the disability centre. With this one and only chance I wailed my nuts off. After all, I was injured and wasn't making this up. I talked about my hand injury, foot injury, head injuries and the failed back, my current predicament and the assortment of other injuries, all with continuing verbal support from the lady from the disability centre, who gave her time for free. They listened intently and then murmured bla bla bla whilst looking down at me, then bla bla bla some more.

I was told to go back to the waiting room while they decided my fate, and, to be honest, I was worried that they would just say no. I know I'm entitled to help but what if I didn't get it, what if they assumed I was just another lying little shit trying to screw the system as many do.

Well, I must have done something right because I was granted Disability Living Allowance for my injured spine. I was already receiving Industrial Injuries Benefit for my foot injury and Income Support and getting these benefits started the whole healing process off because without them I was doomed.

It was also explained to me that I was entitled to a Mobility car, which made my day. The new income was quite considerable compared to the pittance I was living on before, and it was back-dated to 1994, the year of the operation, but not 1990 when I first injured my back. I was just relieved to have actually got the bastards to pay me anything. I felt that this was indeed a result, but also that I had been cheated.

I was also allowed to join the Blue Badge scheme, which meant free parking, along with free rude comments from the passing nosy public, which at first I took quite badly and would always let off a volley of well aimed abuse. In time, I learned to ignore these jibes, but I did stop parking in disabled bays. The main reason was to avoid the amount of questioning from the general public because I don't look that disabled.

Stage Two...Motability Car

On receiving my first cheque, I opened a building society account and stared at my paying in book with disbelief as it was quite a sum in comparison to the income I had to live off before. I ventured to the local Vauxhall car dealership looking for the ideal Motability car. After a few hours I picked one, mainly due to the help given to me by Ray Johnson, who really shone amongst the Swiss Tonies of the motoring world.

In my hours of overexcitement, I chose the wrong car, as I found it very difficult to get in and out of it without severe pain. I should have gone for the MPV, but this way I had a brand new car! I had never owned a brand new car before, and it had matching wing mirrors, another first. I was so proud I was forever polishing it.

Having a car costs quite a large chunk of my benefit, but without transport life with these injuries would really be hard. With our crap government closing our local supermarket to build flats and the local launderette becoming a kebab shop, I have no choice but to travel a few miles to the next town. Now, thanks again to our bloody government, petrol has got so expensive that owning a car is a luxury I really cannot afford. I have to have one, though, as without it I am buggered. I have to mention Motability, who have been exceptional.

Stage Three...Gym

I then joined a gym to strengthen my feeble body as I had lost my Adonis physique! Not just mentally weak, I was also physically very weak. I joined the cheapest gym in Northolt and just went for it. It bloody killed me, especially the rowing, but I had to do this to strengthen the muscles around my lower back. It also helped with sleep. At first I went a couple of times per week and found it very hard work and my pains worsened but in time my strength started to improve; so too my physique. Too often I just didn't want to go because of the pain but knew I had to endure this. I made plans to do up to three months of the year, with the same dull routine, first rowing to strengthen my spine, then static cycling for cardiovascular, and then static weights. I kept this up for many years and I still go, but relapsed last year because of other health issues that needed my attention.

I changed gyms and started at Fitness First in Pinner where I gave myself a similar routine. Yes, it included the bloody rowing machine ,which really hurt, but if I don't work hard my pains worsen, my weakness becomes intolerable, and even climbing stairs becomes hard.

So having rowed four thousand meters, it's then on to several static weight machines, ten repetitions on each machine repeated three times, then the steam room, shower, go home and collapse, knowing that I still have my afternoon walk with the dogs to do. By the time I get home from all that, I am completely shattered, but the endorphins kick in and life becomes a little more pleasurable and just doing this workout makes me feel less disabled and more able.

I push myself hard and have to continue being strict with myself, especially when I really cannot be bothered or the pain becomes just too relentless. The pain does continue but I feel a lot stronger and look better. Not many people with this kind of spine injury would even contemplate putting themselves through so much pain, but I am determined as I am never ever going to give in to this injury.

As I no longer worked I didn't need to eat like a whale, nor for that matter could I afford the plankton. I went from one or two full breakfasts to just eating cereals, and instead of stuffing my face with another massive meal at lunchtime, I ate one or two sandwiches, followed by a banana, an orange and apple. I drank tap water, and in the evening I would eat a proper dinner. I was told that while I am expending so much energy at the gym and walking, I must eat more, and more often. They call this grazing, and I just happen to be an expert at it. This year I signed up for a year, which is a first. I'm proud that I managed to do four months before I had to take a month off. I had pushed far too hard, but I'm back again now, just twice a week and that's perfect, so it's very important to pace oneself.

Stage Four...The Drugs Don't Work

Giving up on all the drugs… Well believe this or not, the legal substances were a lot harder to give up than the illegal ones that I had been shoving into my body for countless years without stopping, asking myself why, just robotically doing as I was told by my, 'couldn't give a toss doc.' The hardest drug to give up was the sleeping pills, as I was almost addicted to them, it took over three months of very cold turkey and very little sleep. I then gave up painkillers, followed by the anti-depressants and finally the anti-inflammatory drugs.

I then chose to stop drinking alcohol, which was a lot easier than I had imagined. One reason was that I stopped going to the pub.

Lastly, I gave up the very illegal but very therapeutic dope which had been a loyal friend for many years. Giving up smoking dope was also a lot easier than I could have ever believed it could be. One day I smoked and the next day I didn't.

It didn't take too long but with the help of the gym and walking, my fitness soon returned and I started to feel and look a tad better than the spotty, underweight knuckle-dragging, disheveled wreck that I had become.

Sometimes, I would wake from a dreamless state, and without thinking, I was reaching for the pills, which turned a good, positive, quite happy me into a dull, grey, uninterested-in- life train crash. I hated them and hated the fact that the doctors would just hand out these useless smarties without once giving a toss about how I felt. I had to man up and I had to do it straight away.

I also stopped talking to the fridge. I succeeded because I just wanted to . I was just not prepared to spend the rest of my life attached to my own weakness.

Wreck...

While my talents neglect me
My broken body is wracked in pain
My thoughts are always yesterday
And where I walk it rains
I have a thousand different memories
That drip from bloodied skies
And a thousand different excuses
To want to run away and hide
So I hide beneath my weakness
In a hole that's under the floor
Where I question my troubled existence
Then I question myself some more
I shout but hear no echo
Feels safe behind these walls
No light coming through my darkness
No life coming through at all.

Stage Five...Goodbye My Friends

The decision about my so-called friends was made a lot easier by their complete lack of interest when I was hanging on so precariously to life. I didn't ask for anything and nor did I receive anything. A bit of support or a friendly arm around the shoulder might have aided a quicker and perhaps, happier recovery, instead of the behind-the-back slagging off and nasty rhetoric, which none of them had the balls to say to my face. These were so-called friends whom I had known for over thirty years. I expected better and it hurt, but realistically, I guess I also knew deep inside the frailty and weakness of these so-called close friendships as they had all let me down before. One friend (let's call him Joe) sort of summed up what I had thought.

It was after a particularly difficult two-hour session at the Pain Clinic where I had received all the paperwork regarding my first five years in the children's hovel and my birth mother. Elaine and I had trawled through the material with the help of a social worker for almost two hours; it was not an easy two hours that's for sure.

I took all the paperwork home and was sifting through it again and I must admit to feeling a tad hacked off and very emotional at its sad contents. Suddenly, there was a knock on my door. I really didn't want to be disturbed as I felt like shit and extremely vulnerable, but I also felt that perhaps a friendly face might help my mood. How wrong I was!

He came in, looked at me, and said sarcastically,

'Having a bad day Kim?'

'Yeah, you could say that. I received some painful news about my childhood,' I replied, waving the reams of paperwork in his general I-don't-give-a-toss direction. Joe turned on me, pointing his finger at my face, and said in a loud and aggressive voice,

'You don't know what pain is Kim. My wife knows what real pain is when she has her periods'.

At first I was just stunned at this careless remark, but then I got angry as I always assumed that he was one of my better friends. He also knew a bit about my life, so to come out with such cold hearted rhetoric was just unbelievable, painful and uncaring. He soon left.

To me that was the end of that long, and I thought, really close relationship.

There were other friends and relationships that also needed to be sorted with a strong mind. One by one I looked at these and soon realized that there probably wasn't the strong link that perhaps I had thought there was, or craved and perhaps hung on to. It didn't take me long to realize that I was no longer wanted and maybe had not been wanted for some time. They all had others in their lives and I don't think that I was going to be in their future plans. Once the decision was made, I never contacted them again.

I knew that my paranoia was again proved correct when one of my best friends dropped dead and I wasn't informed for seven days. If their friends had really wanted to contact me it wouldn't have been that difficult. I was considerably hurt, but I wasn't going to be upset or hurt again. I had to move on.

Stage Six... In the Company of Dogs

Meanwhile, in the land of the living, pissed off, angry, hurting, rejected, abandoned, unsure, uncertain, fearful, despondent, searching, hopeful and bitter, a light still shone from within me. As I had plenty of time on my hands, I decided that I would get myself a rescue dog which was without doubt one of the best moves I have ever made.

My first dog was a rescue, a cross Rottweiler / Doberman bitch, and I chose her because she was a beaten wreck. Her owner left the Mother and puppies locked in a cupboard and the Mother went berserk killing some of her pups. This little three-month old had survived with terrible physical and mental scars and large chunks missing from her ears. As I walked into the sea of Dobermans and Rottweilers, this little face appeared in the corner. I turned to look at her; the face disappeared, only to re-emerge seconds later. I looked over again, and again the face disappeared. I walked over to see this little black and tan puppy. I knelt down beside her and she jumped all over me. 'This is the one for me,' I thought, as I looked into those deep brown eyes. Karen, my landlady, paid the sixty pounds to the Doberman Rescue and off we went, really not realizing just how important this small, beaten dog was going to be to me. I called her Pod and she would change my life forever.

To come home to a tail-wagging, smiling dog waiting for me by the door made me feel warm inside and wanted. Through her love for me I was able to remove a lot of the negatives in my life.

Some years later I got her a friend in the shape of a puppy Rottweiler I called Purdy. This really, really hacked Pod off and I was so concerned that I took a trip to the vet, who told me that she was just jealous. In time she took to the new dog and they played happily together.

My life was beginning to take some sort of shape and I was beginning to feel a lot happier and really enjoyed the company of dogs. Sadly, Pod began to gain weight, so off to the vet, who told me that she needed an ECG and that I could pick her up a bit later on. Four hours went by and I drove back to the vet's to hear the news. It wasn't good. Pod had a leaking heart, but I could take her home for the weekend.

'What do you mean, the weekend?' I asked incredulously.

The vet looked sheepish and nervous when he told me that 'a leaking heart cannot be repaired.'

I took her home for her last weekend alive.

The weekend passed far too quickly, and as I drove her and Purdy to the vet's, I tried to remember all the good things that we had shared and how she had given me the strength to carry on when my life fell apart.

I got to the vet's but he wasn't there and I had to be seen by some irritating gobshite of a woman who had about as much sympathy as gangrene. I laid Pod on the floor, put my arms around her and just wept uncontrollably as the vet put her to sleep with a lethal overdose.

She died instantly.

I stood up and tried to gather myself together. I was weeping and shaking and I just didn't want to leave her. I opened the door to a deathly silent waiting room, where five or six people sat with their pets. They had heard every word, every tearful emotion that I had howled.

I sat in my car crying rivers when there was a knock on the window. It was a woman from the waiting room and she tried to comfort me, but this just made me worse. I drove home with tears streaming down my face. How I didn't crash is a miracle.

Two weeks later I picked up a little coffin for Pod and handed over a month's income. I cradled it in my arms and again wept like a drain. The next few months were unbearable, but I still had Purdy and we had to carry on.

Then sometime later Purdy got ill. I was sitting in my lounge watching television when I saw out of the corner of my eye his head droop. I went over to him and put my arm around his neck to give his head support. He just buried his head into my shoulder. I knew something was wrong. It was late but I had to do something. I rang my vet, only to be greeted by an annoying answer machine giving me another number to ring. I rang it and was greeted by some right miserable bastard. I explained the situation and he told me to go to the emergency vet's in Northolt and bring one hundred and forty pounds. I explained it was late and that I had no a credit or debit card or the cash.

'Then I cannot help you,' he told me. I put the phone down, and, scared and unsure, I erupted.

Luckily, I did have the cash because the next day I was planning to swap my old mobility car for a new one and had the deposit ready. So with money in my pocket and rage in my mind, I headed off to Northolt. I gently put Purdy in the car. He was hardly moving. Deep inside I knew this was going to be his last journey.

I banged on the vet's door. It was opened by a young looking bloke and I just let rip.

'I phoned you half an hour ago; you told me that you wouldn't help my dog unless I had money. Well, here's the money, and here is my dog!

'I'm sorry, I was wrong, come in,' the kid interrupted me in mid rant.

We walked into a small room and I explained Purdy's symptoms. He said that he would put a needle into Purdy's spleen. If it came out with blood in it, there was nothing more that could be done. If it came out clean then there must be another reason.

The syringe was full of blood.

I put my arms around Purdy's neck and hugged him as the vet injected him with a lethal overdose.

Purdy died instantly.

I stood up shaking and handed over the wad in my pocket and walked out. I got in my car and just fell apart. Going home to an empty house for the first time in ten years was loneliness personified. Two very lonely weeks passed and I was back again picking up his little coffin and handing over yet more money.

I thought about life without a dog and decided that I would rather be dead. I made the decision that I had to get another dog and within forty-eight hours I had met yet another rescue dog. I visited him every day for three weeks, which got me out of my lonely home, and of course I met the lovely kennel maids. Being around dog people kept my spirits up as I was missing Purdy so much.

Dogs had become such an integral part of my life. I felt good with them. They just wanted a few basic things from life and what would I do without one? I wouldn't walk miles per day; I couldn't live alone as the company of dogs was far better than the company of some of my so-called friends. You see, dogs really never let you down.

The new dog was a Rottweiler cross/ American Mastiff who I named Little Bear. He wasn't little nor was he a bear, but he was the most gentle and loving dog and really suited my needs. There was something that clicked between us; dog owners would understand this strange comment. Soon I was to take him home, and again my home was less lonely.

Six months later I got yet another dog from the same rescue centre and this one was only a puppy, yet another Rottweiler cross with either a Rhodesian ridgeback or Yeti. Bear now had a good friend to play with, one I called Big Foot. Soon life was back to a kind of normality, and going out every day lifted even the gloomiest days and moods. I never feel lonely or unloved in the company of dogs. They really have helped me in so many ways. I guess they are not called man's best friend for nothing.

Stage Seven...From Abuse to Healing

I began to think about the past abuses in my life and this time it wasn't the physical ones. I wanted to find out more about sexual abuse, so mentally I went back in time to my days in the children's home and tried desperately to remember anything that seemed out of the norm. Everything that had happened there seemed normal until it was recounted from a different perspective. I searched into the dark past and chinks of light emerged from the darkness, the nightmares, the things that happened after dark when I was in bed alone and vulnerable. Did someone come into my room and molest me? Did somebody abuse me sexually? Was something inserted into me? The questions kept coming but no answer until I took it upon myself to delve a little deeper. Some of the nightmares also become clearer when I stood near fat sweaty men, or was that just the normal response? The smell was repugnant, I felt ill, and when very young I also had a jolt when I walked past a black man on a crowded train. The smell reminded me of something but I was still unsure of what.

I have always had a fear of strangers and been homophobic but never knew why. It dawned on me that perhaps these smells and fears were somehow linked to my past. Why, for instance, would I be homophobic? Why my repulsion at fat sweaty men who leered menacingly at me? Why did I find being touched by any men threatening and repulsive, why? If I was in a pub and an openly gay man smirked at me, I would find it unsettling and would avert my eyes, and often feel hostility towards him. What was I so frightened of? What he may think was just being friendly, I didn't. I felt these advances towards me horrible and unsettling and did not like them. Even when an old and trusted friend once put his hand on my knee to help him stand, I felt uneasy. The picture was getting clearer. I was frightened of being touched by men - and I still am.

I still had to explore my own sexuality. I am not gay and I do not find men attractive in a sexual way. I wouldn't want to have sex with a man; I liked to have sex with women, end of story. So with that emotion sorted, I had to venture deeper and that meant only one thing. I had to relive the experience, however dark it might be. If I found the reason, I would find the solution. In short, I had to travel backwoods to go forwards.

What I did is private and will stay private, but I needed to do this. I still feel deeply repulsed by what I did to myself, though one day whilst physically exploring this dark past there was a kind of epiphany. I somehow remembered this feeling and I also recognized the excruciating pain it caused. Was this the memory that I was so desperately searching for? Had I at last found the feeling / sensation that I longed to remember? I felt sick and I felt repulsed but I still had to deal with it, but then it got decidedly worse when I started to self-abuse, (and again what I did remains private), resulting in immediate treatment at the A & E department at Northwick Park Hospital. What I had done to myself could have killed me. I had to stop this self-hate and its vile self-abuses but was this self-hate or was it the memory of sexual abuse? Well, without regression I guess I will never know. If it was self-hatred, then I had to find the cure and begin to love myself, or at least begin to like myself. In time, I did regression with my hatred and fears of homosexuals. Trying to unravel the past and understand its pains and what I believed to be the truth helped in my recovery.

So another problem ticked off the long list and yet another mountain conquered. Goodbye to yet another nightmare and hello to the acceptance of past pains.

Battle...

> My life was a thousand fragments
> That lay scattered across the floor
> I could run and chase daydream fantasies
> Or I could face my one man war
> So prepared I charged into battle
> Screaming an ear-piercing roar
> I'm going to pick up the pieces
> To make me a man once more

So I fight my war like a warrior
Mind fixed at the problem at hand
I will conquer my one man battle
As losing is not part of the plan.

Stage Eight...Forgive Them

Forgiveness was a test I wasn't looking forward to as there seemed to be a never ending streams of people I had to forgive to aid in my battle for self-healing. I had to start with my birth parents.

One night, when I still used to have a joint or two for its therapeutic help, I closed my eyes and drifted off into a trance. I walked into a room where both my birth parents were. I had to make up how they looked as I really had no idea, so I chose Elvis Presley and Mae West. I stood in front of both these strangers, told them my name and that I was their son all grown up, content with life and doing alright.

I turned to my birth Father and verbally laid into him, told him exactly what I thought of him.

'You had sex with my Mother, and in her hours of great need you ignored her pain her suffering, her cries for help and the child she was carrying. You threw them out of your home on to the cold streets of London with no money, no job and no help, you useless worm! Get out of my sight and if I ever have the misfortune see you again I will slot you!' I screamed. Poor old Elvis!

His head bowed with embarrassment, he began to walk meekly out of the room. Before he left I physically and quite aggressively turned him around and held my hand out to shake his. I gripped his feeble, weak, wet hand, looked him straight in the eye and said, ' I forgive you.'

I then turned to my birth Mother and told her that I had missed her, missed all the things a child required, the hugs, the kisses, the attention, being tickled, being bathed, put to bed, read fairy tale stories, to be breast fed, her scent, her warmth, her humour, her laughter and her tears, and that I especially missed her on my birthdays and at Christmas and, worst of all, that I missed being loved. I told her that I knew that she had had a tough time but thanked her for not aborting me and carrying me for nine months, so at least I could be born and that I never held any anger at all towards her, only sympathy and a son's love. I put my arm around her, whispered, 'Goodbye' and left. She said nothing.

The weight I had felt around my shoulders dissipated. I felt no more angst towards either of them. The suitcase packed with all my sadness, which I had carried from one year to the next, started to disappear.

Pandora's Box...

> There sits a lonely suitcase
> At the bottom of my bed
> Inside it hidden treasures
> All the detritus from within my head
> It's there every bloody morning
> When I climb out of my pit
> There sits Pandora's odious box
> Still full of yesterday's shit.

There was still a lot more to forgive. I cast my mind back to my childhood, reminding myself of some of the cruel times with my adopted Mother, not just being hit but other cruelties; the talking about me in a strange language, which I have mentioned earlier whilst I was in the room; forcing me to eat food I found disgusting, and if I refused, it would be kept overnight for me to eat in the morning, cold prunes and custard with a three inch skin.

The unbearable strictness regimes and the many false accusations of lying and theft, not to mention the physical hurt.

Not turning up at my junior school for an exhibition of my expertise in the gym when all the others kids' parents were there. I desperately scanned around the hall but couldn't see mine.

This had a detrimental effect on my schooling and I always seemed to be the only kid who was trawled off to the headmaster to be caned across the palms of my hand or across my bared bottom.

If I was in trouble at school, then I would be in trouble at home, and when I was in trouble at home I would then be in trouble at school. What a completely screwed up cycle of abuse! I could probably write an entire chapter about this woman but I think it's best to leave it there.

My Father never hit me but then he never hugged me either. They were both unemotional and detached.

So again I had to dig deep and say that I forgave them, but this didn't stop some of my negativity towards them.

I was often sent away to summer camps on my own, which I felt at the time was further rejection, but I did learn many skills, so I was really very grateful to them both. I just couldn't get rid of the feelings of being sent away because I was unwanted and not up to the standard that they expected from me, especially the high standards of my siblings who, it appeared, could do no wrong. I was, after all, from a different tribe. I was an uneducated shit, and they were very smart and musical way above average. I couldn't hum in tune although I did try the guitar and while they all were credited for the beautiful music that floated from their bedrooms, I was always admonished for the racket that came from mine. I honestly believed that I was just useless.

Don't think for one minute that forgiveness came easy. It didn't. When I think about what both my Mothers had done to me, it still hurts. Let's be brutally honest here, my birth Mother didn't exactly do me any favors except carry me for nine months and share unknown illnesses, including apparently having syphilis and being born with tuberculosis. (I was informed at a much later date that I didn't have syphilis, but that didn't help with my-self-esteem.)

What a journey! It still makes me wonder what would have happened if she hadn't dumped me so unceremoniously in London. Where would that journey have taken me? Would I have had the same weaknesses and fears that I did because of her rejection? I guess I will never know.

I still have trouble getting through just two days of the year - Christmas Day, when everyone is gearing up and conversing about the 'family', and my birthday which is just another sad bloody reminder of that birth, that woman and the lack of empathy and love. Perhaps it's the hoping that one day I will get a birthday card, knowing full well there is not a chance in hell. Forgiveness was the key to my own freedom and happiness. I guess I just had to deal with it in my own quiet private way.

Stage Nine...I Do Have a Brain

Apart from walking the dogs and working out at Fitness First, I began to release my lifetime of self-defeating emotions by writing them down, journaling as it's often called. I soon realised that writing them down in verse was a lot easier and a whole lot of fun, and they literally poured out of my brain and I felt lighter and happier the more emotions I released. Some of these poems were breathtakingly awful, but one or two even had me smiling. Some, of course, left me crumpled in tears.

I was not brave enough to show anyone at first, perhaps I was just too embarrassed. One day I would show the world, not giving a toss what people thought, but that was going to be some time in the future. I was still a new student and was not mentally tough enough to take criticism. I wrote over one hundred poems. I also wrote a small tract, with Elaine's help. I called it 'The Story of Charlie Two Breakfasts' and it included just a few verses. And I was sort of proud but refused steadfastly to show anyone else

I didn't really know what to do with all my verses, whether to bin them or make a book out of them. I decided to make my very own paperback copy, which also included Charlie Two Breakfasts and about fifty verses. I received my first ten copies in print from my printer and was very proud but still a tad embarrassed with their honest content. I did eventually get brave and sent some copies to my two brothers and sister. I wish I hadn't as I got little or no feedback, but I did hear there had been some poems that they enjoyed reading. Well at least they hadn't binned them.

Now feeling very brave, I decided to get my entire collection of verse printed, again including Charlie Two Breakfasts. These had taken me over eight years to compile and I felt a great sense of relief that I didn't feel the need to write anymore. I had achieved the goal I had set out to achieve: to remove just some of the grey shit that had stuck between my ears for far too many years. It was another task completed.

I had already thought about photography but like any beginner, I was crap. Out of one roll of film one or two photos would be quite good, but the rest would be out of focus or had my thumb across the lens or they were just boring. I did, however, have the perfect practice scenario. I had dogs, a beautiful countryside, woods and sunsets (I was a tad too lazy for sunrises). I began to see through the lens the beauty in life that I had ignored whilst working my body into the ground, and in time my photography improved and so too my belief in my abilities.

Photographing people and road signs just weren't for me, so I just kept banging away until I began to feel at ease and could see the picture I wanted. I soon became good enough, or should I say, happy enough to have some of my photos enlarged, framed and then hung on the barren walls of my home. I was so full of my new skills that I even took photographs of friends' dogs and made calendars. These were just OK, but the owners were delighted with them. I still had doubts about my ability but it was a positive move and made tomorrow look a tad brighter.

I also took up Tai Chi but found it too painful. I did learn enough about the ideas and the inner peace that it could bring. I often found myself throwing shapes whilst out with the dogs in the stillness and quietness of the woods, or late at night in the back garden. I still try, and it's highly recommended.

I also started to learn the guitar and every night after my little rest and dinner I would twang away. Sadly, I am no Jimi Hendrix.

These are just some of the things I listed as 'what I would like to do if possible' all those years ago to begin the healing process. One by one I am ticking them off. I have to keep busy because when I get bored I am a bit of a nightmare to be around. The broken jigsaw of my life was finally coming together.

Stage Ten...Reassurance

I had spent many years teaching myself not to think too much about tomorrow, next week, next month or even next year. It really had to be a day at a time since thinking too far ahead tended to wind me up, especially the thought of spending yet another day, week, month and, god forbid, lifetime with this chronic pain.

This photography malarkey and dog ownership and walking had at least opened up my horizons a little because I know the pain is going to be there irrespective of what I do, and having positive plans can help, but for now it's still a day at a time. I decide what I am going to do when I am walking the dogs in the morning. If I go to bed thinking too much, I don't sleep, so while I walk through the fields near my home, dodging the cow shit, I contemplate life.

Without pushing myself to do this, I really do become a blob of useless cack, so I just keep going, and when the pain just gets too much and I feel I cannot take it anymore, I just calm myself with deep breathing exercises. I remind myself of exactly how far I have come since my close encounter with death and living life stuck in that odious shit pit. I just have to continue with the positive measures that I have taken to ensure a better life for myself and continue to tick off all the jobs on my to-do list. I constantly remind myself that I have achieved a lot.

When I am wet, cold and thoroughly pissed off whilst walking my dogs in the middle of a winter's day, and unhappy that my cave is also cold and I can't afford to heat it, I know, however, I can still hold my head up high because not many people would or could do this especially with my injuries. Not many people could fight as hard as I have done and rest assured, I will never, ever give in and start feeling sorry for myself.

I gave all the bad things that were destroying my life a good old-fashioned kick in the head and I also tamed and came to terms with this never-ending pain by not running away from it. I confronted every weakness and turned it around. I turned all my negatives into positives and have grown to think that I'm all right, far removed from the self-loathing, self-abusing, pained and insecure shadow of a man I used to be. I have also been able to forgive all the people who chose to make my life hell as nearly all the problems that I have encountered throughout this life, from birth to now, was the result of other people's selfishness and greed.

Stage Eleven...Oh You Bastard Pain

Dealing, coping, understanding, accepting and living with constant pain for the rest of my life seemed like an impossible task. How wrong was I? This didn't happen overnight. In fact, it took ages and I will explain the route I took.

I first started to realize and understand that whatever happens to me, this pain will be with me until I die or until the NHS starts to perform miracles or indeed offer me an operation you can easily have, if you pay for it. The removal of my pain starts in the mind. I have endured many physical pains before and beaten them, and addressing this one was not going to be any more difficult than the others.

Everything starts with acceptance of the pain. Knowing the pain and understanding exactly how it arrives. What does what to what to result in this agony? Why does it hurt so much more late at night and first thing in the morning? Why does it hurt so much doing the simplest things like sitting hour after hour writing all this crap on my computer?

With all the will in the world, I cannot stop bone rubbing on bone, nor can I stop nerves being crushed resulting in spasms of extreme pain. I could help myself by not making the situation worse, bending, stretching, lifting awkward weights like shopping, any sudden movement, driving or sitting for too long, having sex, washing, putting on my socks and underwear. In fact, putting underwear on is almost humorous and now and again I find myself in fits of the giggles as I try in vain to do the simplest tasks. Of course, there are also times when it does get the better of me. This is not good since, at the beginning of the day when you really want to be as cheerful as possible, bending over the wash basin for my morning ablutions wasn't easy. I had to raise the basin by six inches. I chuckle that I should have made it two feet.

One thing that I do when the pain is extreme is to imagine myself lying on a beautiful sandy beach, with a turquoise sea, on a hot day surrounded by lovely large-breasted women, as you can imagine, I am not thinking about my pain.

A hot bath does wonders as it isn't weight bearing. Lying down on a comfortable couch propped up with a multitude of pillows (when in bed put a pillow between your legs, trust me it does help), relaxing and not being stressed, listening to some soothing music and putting away Black Sabbath for another time. And, if you can, try Tai Chi. It does help, although you will feel a tad stupid when you do it for the first time in your back garden as the neighbours stare wondering if you're having a fit.

I did, as you know, smoke the odd joint and this is a great way to 'get away' from the pain. Sadly though, the sudden impact of coming back to earth with all its gravity and misery tends to make the reality of life even more unbearable and the journey to Planet Zanusi even nicer. It's a difficult one. If you do choose the drugs route, ask yourself, are you going to spend the rest of your days running away from the real issue of pain or are you going to stand still and fight? I thought that I would miss it, but I just don't…well, ok, just sometimes.

Another way to deal with pain is to read about how other people deal with their own sufferings, soldiers, for instance, and amputees and burn victims. If you have a relative who has been through extremes of pain, you must learn and not be afraid to ask them and find out more.

Pain also brings with it other unseen problems such as stress.

I read somewhere that chronic pain is a chronic form of stress, so on top of having to deal with the day-to-day hassles we all have to face, you also have to deal with the stress of never-ending pain. It is, however, part of our lives. If, for instance, you are going to be involved in a head-on collision your body readies itself for something called stress response. (Yes, I read this somewhere, probably waiting in the pain clinic).

Increased blood supply to arms and legs is what happens.. Remember flight or fight? This can make you feel shaky, increase your heart rate and breathing, make your stomach turn into a spinning tumble dryer as blood is diverted from digestive duties to arms and legs. Dizziness also occurs as blood is diverted from your panicking brain to arms and legs. There's also sweating and dilation of pupils to increase vision. These responses are all great in an emergency situation, but they are about as much use as udders on a bull when you are not in danger.

Now, as I am in smug, smart-arse Doc Kim mode, I shall continue in this clever vein and bang on about the nasty evil vicious cycle *you* are in.

Stress leads to tension, which leads to pain, which leads to depression, which leads to anger, which leads to stress. Fucking hell! But if you're relaxed then you cannot be tense. Relaxation also helps with disturbed sleep patterns, and if all else fails, you can always try hypnosis.

Your Pain Clinic or GP can give you piles of reading matter regarding all these irritants. I suggest you read them, and then read them again and again until you know exactly what you need to do to solve these countless problems. It may just change your life. You may become a totally different person and if you succeed, you will probably come out of this a much nicer, cool dude, just like me!

Now think about these…

*Unrealistic thoughts lead to worry, catastrophic over-generalization, and selective attention, emotional reasoning which are giving an inaccurate picture of your problems.

*Worrying, thinking about a problem that doesn't exist and is not important.

*Catastrophising is making a mountain out of a molehill.

*Over-generalization…You think just because one problem went tits up, the rest will obviously follow. It doesn't.

*Selective attention; doing something positive and then knocking it, such as I did… well today, but I did get help.

*Emotional reasoning; for instance, I am hopeless today so tomorrow I will be hopeless again. This is just negative. What I say is, 'I was hopeless yesterday, no fucking way am I going to be hopeless today.'

As I stated earlier, this all takes time and all your problems cannot be sorted out in a few days. Take your time, avoid hurry sickness (hoping today was already over) and day by day you will grow stronger. Yes, there will be days when you feel and probably are useless and pathetic, but remember that today will soon be over and tomorrow is another day with yet another chance to be a tad braver and a tad more resilient.

Another idea is to have a goal, something to look forward to that doesn't have to be reached by a time limit. You are not at work now. I set myself tasks to complete when I am ready. I do not rush into any of them. I will get it done in my own time. It might just be a trip to the library and perhaps a walk in the afternoon. After all, we're not joining the SAS. Then tomorrow, flushed with the success of today, you can push that bit harder, or if you prefer, do diddly squat.

You must remember not to give in. After a while you may feel so good and smug about yourself that you may want to try more exercise, such as swimming, static cycling and some repetition exercise down the gym.

You must remember to relax as much as possible, to sit or lie down, have a nice hot cup of tea.

Try your deep breathing exercises, sit in the garden, but please do not fall into the trap of going backwoods into depression and despair as this will make the next step harder, not easier.

I said earlier that I felt that I was at the bottom of a pit and every day I climbed a little higher. Do not allow despair to reappear as you will quickly slide back down into the odious shit pit again.

You will find that everything starts to improve, your attitude, your sleep patterns, your looks, your general outlook on life, so when you are having a good day enjoy the sod because tomorrow might not be as good and you'll have to work even harder. Keep this up for the amount of time that I have had to (over eighteen years) and you too can be full of yourself, as I say with humour.

Perhaps in time you can also help others who need your knowledge and experiences. You will be astounded at how far you have come since your injury and subsequent operations. It's ok to remind yourself of this and I certainly do. I think about the time in hospital when I begged the invisible God to let me die because I just couldn't see a way out of my problems. I didn't believe that I had the ability to succeed when all the odds were stacked up against me. Well, I did succeed! Do I feel proud? Yes, just a bit.

So that's some of the crap that I have endured and what I did to overcome these issues. You can see that I am obviously an expert, and that the sun does actually shine out of my arse! I will now make some positive suggestions for you, starting with...

Stage Twelve...Physical Injuries...and How to Cope

Well, congratulations on your brand new injury and hopefully that the NHS has somehow mended you to the best of their abilities, not left you up shit creek like they had me on so many occasions, (no not bitter or twisted at all). What they don't do, however, is tell you how to deal with the daily pain and instead you will have been given a cupboard full of nasty drugs to be taken up to four times per day, (at my worst I was on sixteen a day, seven days a week for what seems an eternity). All of them were crap, which brought my normal abilities to 'self-heal' crashing through the floor. With them came self-doubt, depression and anxiety.

Dependency will soon follow, so ensure that you really need painkillers before you start gulping them down because my belief, and I speak from vast experience, is they just don't stop the pain. I have not taken any for eons as I have learned that I am the only one who can control this. You also need to learn how to accept the pain. You have to teach yourself to be stronger than your pain and that you can take it. Don't curl up sloth-like and give in. You will be amazed at how tough and resilient you, your body and mind are. Be bloody-minded about it, and if you think you're a tough guy, bloody prove it and don't be a Sissy Mary.

Pain-killers just cut off some off your senses and overnight you will turn into a dribbling, drooling, useless, bed-wetting waste of space. That might be all right for a week or two, but not for any serious length of time as you will turn into a Zombie and perhaps start to look like one as your feeding habits will change and also your sleeping habits.

This brings me nicely to sleeping pills, which are also useless. They, too, will leave you dazed and confused. You will not awake refreshed singing the joys of the world; instead you will feel like you're dead. You don't get a good night's sleep; you just get knocked out, with no more lucid dreams, no lovely warm cozy feelings. One minute you're awake, the next you wake up and wonder what happened to the night. Then you're going to take your painkillers and the cycle begins again.

One day you will have to give them all up as you cannot take them forever. You will then suffer from withdrawal symptoms (cold turkey) which I can tell you is hell. There's no sleep, but maybe, if you are very lucky, you might get the odd hour here and there. You will lie awake at night, trying to sleep. The harder you try, the longer you stay awake. You can always try the 'staying awake way' in which you do just that; try to keep awake in the hope that you will fall asleep (it didn't work for me). This could send you round the bend and, of course, no sleep will leave you pissed off, tired and very angry as you have been feeding your body a whole ton of shit. I can say in all honesty and with some bad language, treat these two drugs like the plague they are.

Most pain is hard to deal with at first as it's so in your face. Everything you do hurts and you just don't know how to deal with it. I have a simple answer to this, which may sound stupid, but you must remember I have been in physical pain with just my back injury since 1992, not forgetting the foot injury and before that my hand injury and head injuries. I do know what I'm talking about.

The thing you have to do is 'ignore it', however hard that might seem at first. You can do it. Think of something else to keep yourself occupied. I walked my dogs, and at first the pain was incredible, but if you teach yourself not to think about it, to tell your body and mind that you are not in pain, you will conquer it. If you have ever suffered real pain, you will know how bad it can be. I will have this knife-lodged-in-my-spine pain for the rest of my life, and I have to be positive, strong and self-disciplined every day. This type of pain can destroy even the strongest people. My suggestions are to strengthen the weakness - yes, like using a rowing machine.

You can imagine that it feels like my spine is being ripped out of my back, but the strength you get, the endorphins that come crashing all around you, and the fact that you're doing something positive about it will make you feel very good about yourself. Of course, you can just give up, sit in a wheelchair and let everybody feel sorry for you, get people to wait on you hand and foot, moan to your heart's content, take all the legal / illegal drugs and alcohol that you can get your hands on, and waste the rest of your life. It's really up to you. Every day I keep repeating to myself, 'These injuries will never ever beat me.'

Then get a good Doctor. I can tell you in all honesty that this is about as easy as herding plankton. I spent many years under some right horrible heathens. Eventually, I did get the Doc I needed to help with my particular problems. Don't think that you have to just accept anybody you have been given. Exercise your rights no matter how irritating you may become and how tiresome it is.

Keep banging on that door until you are happy and when you have found the Doc of your dreams, hang on to him/her like a limpet mine. You also have to then tackle the government benefit system. I wish you all the luck in the world. You'll need it and medication. Be cool and expect Muppets; you have rights and entitlement, so don't give up and just keep banging away. Mine only took two and half years, so no stress there then!

Don't think because you're going through hell that anybody really gives a toss. The chances are that they won't; this sounds a tad harsh and bitter, but sadly it's true. You can tell a story just once. You tell the same story ten times and suddenly you're alone while your so-called loved ones and friends are bored rigid of the noise, your wailing drone of self-pity. This pain or injury may be tough for you, but it isn't tough for them as they are not going through your problems. You can rest assured that when they get a tenth of what you're suffering they will whine like a castrated pig for weeks. The best thing to do with your new found pain is just take it and keep the waffle to a minimum.

When you have finally come to terms with the fact that there is something very wrong with your life, don't hide it in that odious suitcase - that odious suitcase with all its sad emotions will be there tomorrow and the day after. Confront the bastard from within, admit the problem.

Don't keep running away. STAND STILL, GET HELP.

If, like I did, you are searching the past to help with your future. there is a bit of advice regarding searching for birth parents.

Please be careful because your birth parents may not want you back, and just turning up may do both of you more harm than good. The question you should ask yourself is, 'Could I handle being rejected a second time?' Imagine receiving a letter asking you to keep the hell away. Chances are that this may well happen. The best bet is to go to agencies which deal with this kind of situation on a daily basis. After all, you're not alone. There are many people who undergo searches of this kind.

When I began to search for my past I went to NORCAP and they were superb. Although I wasn't searching for my birth family, they were really very helpful with all manner of issues. There is also a company (name escapes me) which will put your name on a file so that if anybody wishes to find you or has been looking for you, this company can give you the information. I think it cost £15. I put my name down to see if anybody had asked after me. Sadly, nobody had. This stung a little, but like a lot of things you just have to accept that your birth parents may have moved on, probably remarried and had more children. Don't beat yourselves up; you will just have to accept this.

Remember the real pain was a long time ago when you were abandoned. Re-opening this old wound could do irreparable damage to you and your future.

I just accepted that I wasn't wanted. No amount of searching is going to change the minds of your birth family. It's a tough decision but I am sure you can make the correct one.

I didn't suddenly become healed overnight and there is still a lot to learn about myself and life. I continue to make silly errors in judgment, and although I have said that I am a content man, this doesn't necessarily mean that I'm annoyingly happy. What I have achieved is just the ability to come to terms with the life I have with all its foibles. There are still many things that I have would liked.

I have controlled the insanely furious / ludicrously amiable too. I have anger and it's under control. Without this anger I would not have been able to confront many of my issues, and now that is under control. I have a great sense of inner strength and believe I have become unbeatable. I needed to do this. Some people just rely on others. I went the other way and relied on nobody but myself . There is a sense of 'well done' but I don't go overboard with this, I'm all right.

I have also noticed that when I smile and say a cheerful 'hello' I normally get a smile and cheery 'hello' back. I often remind myself to have a good day and smile at life rather than be the brooding bad-tempered, angst-fueled person filled with hate and resentment. I know the world is full of shits, but I also know there are some thoroughly decent people out there, and if people refuse to be nice back, sod them.

I have at last found the correct balance. I sit in the middle of life's seesaw, grinning inanely at how content I have become. My life is still tinged with loneliness and my wishes for company seem to drift away, but I have found the meaning of love and life - love in the shape of my dogs and understanding life in the journey that I lead. I still have a lot to learn. If, like me, you start right at the bottom and you have been given or chosen a difficult journey, I believe the battle and journey will be worth its pain. When you do achieve happiness and peace, it just tastes that little bit sweeter than for those who have been given everything.

So, to finish off, I would just like to add that, although I feel that I have been to hell and back, that I will have to spend the rest of my days in chronic pain, that my solitude is sometimes unbearable, that some days I think about the peace and freedom that awaits me in death, you won't actually find a more content man. I have learned that happiness doesn't begin with money and greed, flash cars and an array of pretty women hanging off my arms like fruit bats hanging off a tree.

If I was offered another hundred lifetimes on this beautiful Planet and do all the things and suffer all the pains again, just to be me, I would probably say a quiet 'yes' but through gritted teeth. I have learned valuable lessons in life.

I probably was always a good guy, but somehow lost sight of this in trying just too hard to belong or to be accepted and a part of somebody's else's life. Too often I found myself saying,'Here I am, somebody notice me.'

Like all apprenticeships, this one takes just a bit longer. What I became after all the wars were over is how I would like to be judged, and not by the many mistakes and the many bad judgments that I have made.

Without this harsh indoctrination I would not have been able to find the ability, strength and sheer determination to deal with the bigger picture called life.

Look at life as a gift.

Think positively about your life and don't be dragged down by overbearing negativity and weakness.

CHAPTER TWENTY TWO
LOOKING FOR LOVE AND FINDING TRUTH

Undeterred, life carries on and with it continuing physical pain, but there was just one pain I really wanted to face, confront and hopefully change and that is the pain of not being or feeling loved by that special someone. I have now been single for over twenty years and not luxuriated in sex in eighteen years. Yes I decided to take some time out but it's becoming a lifetime without love and I needed to change this or find out why I hadn't and wasn't.

To be honest, I decided that, since I don't go out anymore as I don't drink, the type of woman I would like is not one I would meet drunk in a pub. Remember, I have done that and felt more alone than wanted. A friend recommended that I join an online dating site and suggested one. Sadly due to legal reasons I cannot divulge its name so I will make up one; let's call it 'P.L.U.G'. You can make up your own derogative derivations; I know I have. So I joined this 'FREE' online dating site called P.L.U.G and I am automatically asked to fill out a questionnaire. Listed below are some of their questions, plus a few of my own...

My gender

Seeking

Height

I am looking for, (then gives a selection of relationship choices, such as long term, short term, casual or farmyard animal)

Hair colour

Body type

Number of legs

Type of car

Education

Eye colour

Do you want children?

Can you balance a potato on your head?

Do you suffer from creeping alopecia?

Marital status

Do you have children, if so what type?

Do you smoke?

Can you walk upright?

Do you have hairy palms?

Do your knuckles hang closer to your hips or drag along the floor?

Do you live in a tree?

Are you a bonobo monkey?

Do you do drugs?

Do you drink?

Do you have a pet?

What is one plus one?

Are your children hairy?

Can you spell your own name?

By now I was beginning to lose the will to live, let alone answer more inane questions. I tried to skip all the reams of rhetoric but was told in no uncertain terms to complete the 'questionnaire you single sad act'. I meekly obeyed...

When it comes to dating what best describes your interest?

What is the longest relationship you have been in?

Now it gets a tad more interesting as it asks me to write a short or long synopsis about me, i.e., talk about my hobbies, talk about goals and aspirations, talk about yourself and what makes you unique, unique?, I wouldn't be on this odious, cheap, crappy, anally retentive dating site, if was unique?

It also has asked me for a username.

I called myself, 'waxmydolphin.' I didn't actually believe that there would be one sane woman in the world who would be in the slightest bit interested in dating a man/ape who called himself 'waxmydolphin'. Oh how wrong was I?

I checked out some of the talent on show and the remains of my libido dropped like a brick thrown from the Eiffel tower. I scoured the hordes of grinning, toothless, overweight harridans looking back at me and felt physically sick.

I returned some hours later to be absolutely stunned that I had about ten messages. I quickly signed in and checked my messages and the hordes of beauties who wanted to date me. I was heartbroken. There wasn't one woman who was younger than I was. Some had fewer teeth than a goldfish; most suffered from creeping alopecia, turtle necks, bingo wings, facial growth; and a few looked like they had applied their make up with a club hammer, chain saw or anvil, or all three. I was utterly despondent.

I turned off the computer and hoped that perhaps in another

day or so I might find what I had asked for. Asked for? I questioned myself, what did I ask for? Did I state you must be younger than God and be less hairy than Harriet the hairy yeti? 'No', I had completely forgotten. So I hastily wrote 'must be between forty and sixty years old, single, attractive and live within fifty miles of London'. I sat back and waited and waited.

I got one message asking the meaning of 'Waxmydolphin' and was it a euphemism?

'No, that's really my birth name' I replied sarcastically.

Soon my inbox was full to bursting and as yet, not one attractive woman; not one even called herself Mad Mary and had tattoos covering her torso and had a face resembling a recently shot baboon.

'Oh god this isn't what I wanted,' I wailed to the computer screen. What did I want, was really the question? I guess I was just lonely and in need of some good company or perhaps I just wanted sex or to have my dulled spirit and machismo rubbed enthusiastically, but this wasn't the way forward. Well not until I got a couple of messages, one from a blond woman who was drop dead gorgeous and came with the name 'Firestarter' and another whose name escapes me. We chatted by email but I was soon put off by Firestarter when she told me she had been asked out by no less than nine hundred men. I decided then and there that I would leave her well alone, but also that I would try again another time, but will explain about that later.

The other woman whose name escapes me seemed very interested, looked very attractive and lived close by, in fact five miles away. We typed, we laughed mostly at different times and we flirted quite openly and sexually, and soon she was sending me her telephone number. I rang and this polite voice replied and the laughing, flirting continued, but something didn't sound right as she stated "fifty year old from Stanmore". Her voice seemed older, a lot older. It was arranged that we should meet and that, as she was a dog owner, we should go for a nice walk in the woods with dogs in tow. Excited by the prospect, I washed my best walking clothes which still made me look like an unkempt tramp. I even brushed the dogs.

Ready for the walk, I did a quick face check in the rear view mirror to detect signs of spots, boogies, unsightly nostril hair and food between the teeth. I drove with my two huge dogs the five miles and soon was parked outside her house. It looked old and unkempt, but undeterred I got out of the car, checked my "garbage," ensuring it was facing the ground and not my head, and walked over and gently knocked on the front door. My two dogs looked on from the open back window of my car.

I had already prepared in my mind that I wasn't going to be rude or say anything dirty or sexual, just to be polite and friendly. I heard the clip clop footsteps; I laughed to myself and muttered, 'Oh Christ, I hope she's not a horse.'

The door creaked open one in old vampire films and there standing in front of me was…. Lazarus. Attached to her arm was a hairy mollusk and in the back ground I could hear what sounded like a lung machine. My mind raced to find adequate words. None came, and even the dogs were now shouting, 'Quick Kim, leg it'.

I looked at the vision that stood before me and noticed she had a camel toe the size of Cheddar Gorge. Looking down, I saw she had gold slip-on slippers. I worked my way quickly past Cheddar Gorge to her ample but rather sagging breasts, quickly looking to the right to see if the hairy mollusk had moved or started to breathe. Then I glanced again at her face; she smiled, her false teeth protruding like an unwanted early morning erection, her face wrinkled and ancient and her eyes glazed with cataracts.

'Oh for the love of God what have I done?' I whispered.

The dogs were trying to lasso me with their leads and for probably the first time in my life, I was lost for words,

'Fifty from Stanmore - more like one thousand and fifty from Jerusalem'.

'Oh hello' I blurted out and almost said, 'Is your great, great, great, great, grand-daughter alive still?'

'You must be Kim,' she said.

'I must be fucking blind,' I replied under my breath.

The hairy crustacean on her arm still hadn't moved.

'Shall we go then?' I asked hoping she had changed her mind,

'Yes, ok but let me get my cardy first', she mumbled as she glided back to her back room, soon to reappear with the hairy wart on her arm that still hadn't moved.

I opened the car door to let her in, placed her coffin and wheelchair, Zimmer frame and an array of walking sticks in the back and we drove off to the woods.

'Does your dog have legs?' I politely inquired,

'Of course it does,' the caustic, spit-ridden hag replied.

We got to the woods and I let the boys out and they ran off at some pace. I marched off at my normal pace only to hear,

'What am I, a fucking Indian?'

'I'm sorry, what did you say?'

'I said, am I a fucking Indian? Slow down,'

I realised that this walk was going to be the shortest in the history of dog walking and the chances of me wanting to clap eyes or hear the foul-mouthed rhetoric pouring from her ugly mouth were pretty slim.

'Are you going to put your dog down?' I asked,

'Nothing wrong with her, why would I put her down?' she cackled.

'No I meant, are you going to let the dog use its legs and actually walk, you hideous harridan?' I whispered.

She knelt down and put the dog on the floor. Soon it was running with my boys and then very soon picked up again.

'Let's go home', I said, realising that we hadn't actually made any conversation whatsoever. I dropped her off at her home and drove back to the woods thinking: never, ever will I do that again.

We never spoke again.

First lesson in online dating, never believe a word they say or the age of the photos or the age they tell you they are.

I went back to P.L.U.G and contacted Firestarter and a dinner date was arranged.

She seemed nice. We swapped telephone numbers and when we did speak she spent the entire conversation talking about her children, zumba dancing, work and sailing on her millionaire friend's boat. I felt disinterested and totally fed up with the entire online dating game. That's what it seemed, a game, and one I wasn't very good at or prepared to join.

I arranged to meet Firestarter the very next Thursday and hurried about trying to find a suitable place to eat that wasn't a beef burger joint or a caravan on bricks. I found a nice curry house and all was arranged, but then she emailed saying,

'Can we make it Tuesday and not Thursday?'

'No, I can't make Tuesday, (I could but I felt she was rushing and probably over booked her nine hundred dates. I was not prepared to be walked over however attractive she was in comparison with Lazarus and her lung machine)

'Perhaps another time when you are less busy.' I replied, she was certainly hacked off about that but I didn't want to be just another sad act date.

We didn't speak again for almost a year. Again we arranged a meet and again it fell through. Two years elapsed but we did keep contact on the phone now and then, and again the conversation was 'my sons this, my sons that, my daughters this, my daughters that, I go dancing three times per week, I go out with my girlfriends twice a week. I see my children all the time, bla bla bloody bla.'

We finally met just over one month ago, almost three years since we first flirted, we had tea and scones, polite conversation and a mutual reality that this was going nowhere. We agreed to keep in contact; we however, have not, which actually is just fine.

I gave up; no more dating, no more achingly ugly Lazarus's pretending to be fifty when in fact they were the same age as the earth. No more women who applied their slap with an anvil, and no more dirty, sex- starved harridans who wanted to meet for sex at some cheap grubby hotel. No, this definitely wasn't for me.

I was lonely; I was looking for love, but not so lonely or desperate that I would mate a chimp in makeup.

I began to realise what I was really looking for. I was looking for lost love, and perhaps the lost love I never had from my birth Mother,or the acceptance I craved from my adopted

Mother. I felt that was never ever going to happen, and that, sadly, that love had passed me by. I must move on.

I have met, been fancied by, and dated many women, but they all came with luggage, children, boyfriends, madness, ex-boyfriends and even husbands. I fell in love and got my heart broken time and time again. I just couldn't take another heartbreak or rejection again. So I finally gave up.

So at fifty eight years of age, twenty one year's single and eighteen celibate, I finally decided, enough was enough. If she arrives without the above luggage and problems, then I will open my door, just a little, but right now, it's sadly and very firmly, closed. You see, I do want that lost love, I yearn for it. I want to be special to someone, but not to be placed in a queue of, 'my children first, then my best friends, then my family, then my work, my nails, my hair and if you are very lucky and grovel daily, you.

I accept that the chances of ever finding this lost love are very slim, but the chances of finding a new love, well I will just have to see.

The final Chapter
So where am I now?

Alone but not necessarily lonely, I have my dogs; I have a few true friends whom I can rely on and trust implicitly. I have my injuries, my paltry benefits, my Motability car, my cold cave, my pain and my memories. I have written and published over one hundred and fifty poems. I have written and published this book, now in a second edition. I have written and published a book about my rescue dogs, and I have written three children's books, two of which are published and the third should be. I also have a dream of self-improvement; I hope one day to earn enough from my books to get off this odious but life-saving benefit system and to be finally free of pain.

Perhaps at last, I finally understand myself, my life and my trials that never seem to stop. Perhaps they never will, perhaps only with death will all pain cease, but while I am standing and still breathing. I will just not allow anything to break or beat me. I have become invincible and unbreakable. Life has done its best to do that and it's failed time and time again. So to everyone who beat me, cheated on me, abused me, hurt me and lied to me - and you know who you are - you have failed. I can stand today and say without any fear that I am proud of who I am, my unknown heritage, my skin colour, my wars of attrition and battles with life itself.

I have loved many people in my varied life and I think,

perhaps hope, that I have been loved back. I am who I am today, unbeaten and unbowed, badly bruised by life but never ever feeling sorry for myself, or seeking the greed and selfishness of so many others.

I am proud of all my achievements, no matter how small and insignificant they may seem to others, since these were not handed down to me on a plate. I have fought for everything and have been fighting since I was abandoned on the 13th August 1954, aged just fifteen days old to face this big frightening, uncaring and unfriendly hostile journey alone…and ultimately… I won… and as for the future?

Well pain continues unabated; issues with my body continue, including a cancer scare last year. There are Achilles heel issues, waiting for an operation for new right hip, waiting for operation for the trigger finger on my left hand. The list continues and will continue as my body is getting older by the day, but luckily, my mind has become unbeatable. And I?

I'm not scared any more…

Amaranta...

> You chased me through the spring meadows of my childhood
> In the warm bird song summer sun
> With you I never had a day of sorrow
> As I look back at what we had done
> I call you Amaranta
> A flower that never fades
> You were my rays of happiness

Through a thousand silent plays
How many words are there to express the way this feels
Even after separation from you I still cried alone in my dreams
So sad I was unable to show you how I felt
Guess it's just the way life was
The cards that we were dealt
I call you Amaranta
My flower that never fades
You were my rays of sunshine
Through a thousand silent prayers
So now as we get older, separation looms again
I just wanted to say to you that you have always been my friend
But I think, no, I know you're so much more than that
A hidden unused word, I think it's just called love
So thank you Amaranta
My flower that never fades
You were my rays of sunshine
Through all my breathing days
I will always love you Amaranta
Until my life force fades away
You are my Amaranta
The flower that never fades.

Index of Poems…

Pg 1)…Abandoned

Pg 4)…Kathleen

Pg 6)…Mother Kathleen

Pg 8)…Ugly Tree

Pg 10)…Brown Skinned Boy

Pg 15)…Don't Hit Mummy

Pg 18)…Dustbin Lid

Pg 28)…Fallen

Pg 84)…Confess

Pg 90)…Stinking Pit

Pg 103)…Shit Creek

Pg 110)…Wreck

Pg 119)…Battle

Pg 122)…Pandora's Box

Pg 151)…Amaranta

Jonny Plumb Series

Title: Jonny Plumb and The Golden Globe
   Author: Kim Wheeler
   Publisher: TotalRecall Publications, Inc.
   Format:
     Paper Back: ISBN: 978-1-59095-186-6
     eBook: ISBN: 978-1-59095-187-3
   Number of pages in the finished book: 130
   Publication Date: April 8, 2014

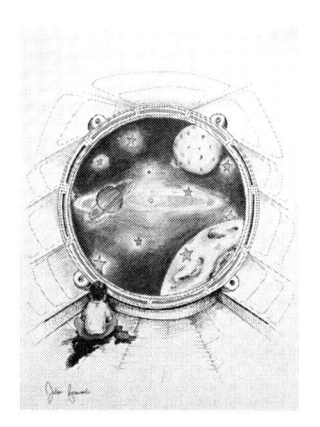

Title: Jonny Plumb and the Silver Space Ship
   Author: Kim Wheeler
   Publisher: TotalRecall Publications, Inc.
   Format:
     Paper Back: ISBN: 978-1-59095-188-0
     eBook: ISBN: 978-1-59095-189-7
   Number of pages in the finished book: 130
   Publication Date: April 8, 2014

Title: Jonny Plumb and the City of Amaranta
   Author: Kim Wheeler
   Publisher: TotalRecall Publications, Inc.
   Format:
     Paper Back: ISBN: 978-1-59095-190-3
     eBook: ISBN: 978-1-59095-191-0
   Number of pages in the finished book: 130
   Publication Date: April 8, 2014

Author: Kim Wheeler

Kim Wheeler was born at University College Hospital, London in 1954 and was promptly abandoned by his birth mother. He was then taken into care by the local authority and moved south of the Thames to a children's home in Lewisham, where he spent the next five years. He was eventually fostered and adopted at age six and moved to Pinner. At the age of eleven he was sent away to a boarding school, which he left it at fifteen, with few qualifications.

Over the next thirty years he suffered from several physical injuries, survived meningitis and, finally disabled with an incurable spine injury, was ordered to cease all types of manual work. Mental health issues and complete breakdown soon ensued.

Kim is also a self-taught photographer, a writer of over one hundred published poems and prose, a dog trainer and dog rescuer. He has also learnt to play the guitar, but sadly the sound he makes resembles a horse eating shreddies.

Despite being battle scarred he refuses steadfastly to be beaten by any of the many trials and continues to face daily battles with all the physical pains without complaint. Through the love and the walking of his rescue dogs, attending the gym, and writing, he has found contentment in his varied life that seemed almost unattainable many years ago...